# WOMEN
# RITES
# &
# SITES

D0140050

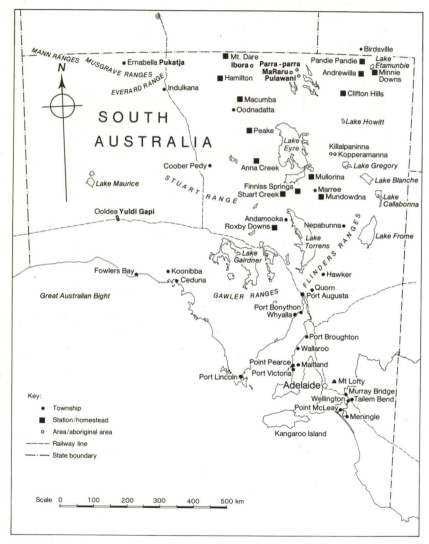

Key:
- • Township
- ■ Station/homestead
- o Area/aboriginal area
- ----- Railway line
- —·— State boundary

Scale  0   100   200   300   400   500 km

South Australia

Aboriginal women's cultural knowledge

# WOMEN RITES & SITES

Edited by Peggy Brock

Allen & Unwin
Sydney   London   Boston   Wellington

Allen & Unwin Australia Pty Ltd
An Unwin Hyman company
8 Napier Street, North Sydney, NSW 2060 Australia

Allen & Unwin New Zealand Limited
75 Ghuznee Street Wellington, New Zealand

Unwin Hyman Limited
15–17 Broadwick Street, London, W1V 1FP England

Unwin Hyman Inc.
8 Winchester Place, Winchester, Mass 01890 USA

National Library of Australia
Cataloguing-in-Publication entry:

Women, rites & sites: Aboriginal women's cultural knowledge.

Includes bibliographies and index.
ISBN 0 04 370186 8.

[1]. Aborigines, Australian – Women. [2]. Aborigines, Australian –
Social life and customs. [3]. Aborigines, Australian – Rites and
ceremonies. I. Brock, Peggy, 1948 –

306'.0899915

Library of Congress Catalog Card Number: 89–83592
Typeset in 10/11 pt Baskerville by Times Graphics, Singapore
Printed by Kin Keong Printing Co, Singapore

# CONTENTS

# ACKNOWLEDGEMENTS

THE ABORIGINAL Heritage Branch of the Department of Environment and Planning in South Australia originally commissioned the reports on which this book is based. The manager of the branch, R. J. Ware, has endorsed the recommendations of those reports and has been an enthusiastic supporter of the publication of the book. Luise Hercus, a contributor, made time available to ensure the orthography of Aboriginal words was consistent. Vlad Potezney drew up the map of South Australia and plotted the locations mentioned in the text and Joan Murray good humouredly assisted with the typing.

# NOTE ON SPELLING

SPELLINGS OF Aboriginal words and tribal groups vary dramatically. Dr Luise Hercus kindly agreed to check the orthography used in eight of the chapters to ensure consistency in this volume. Dr Catherine Berndt has used her own orthography, developed over many years.

Some of the common variations of spellings of tribal names (with Dr Hercus' orthography first) are as follows:

| | | | | |
|---|---|---|---|---|
| Pitjantjatjara | Pidjanjara | Pitjandjara | | |
| Antikirinja | Antingari | Antikirinya | Antakirinja | Andagarinja |
| Kukata | Kokatha | Kokata | | |
| Adnjamathanha | Adnyamathanha | Adnjamatana | | |
| Wangkangurru | Wongkanguru | | | |
| Diyari | Dieri | | | |
| Yankuntjatjara | Jangkundjara | | | |
| Kuyani | Kujani | | | |
| Yandruwantha | Jandruwanta | | | |
| Pirlatapa | Pilatapa | Piladapa | | |
| Yadliyawara | Jadliaura | | | |
| Yawarawarrka | Jauraworka | | | |
| Thirrari | Tirari | | | |
| Ngamini | Ngameni | | | |
| Arrernte | Aranda | | | |

# MAPS

# FIGURES

# CONTRIBUTORS

**Linda Barwick** received her doctorate on Italian traditional song from Flinders University in 1986, and is now a National Research Fellow at the University of New England, where she is collaborating with Professor Ellis on a research project entitled 'Style and Structure in Central Australian Aboriginal Music.' She has published work in the fields of women's studies, television and Italian culture in Australia, as well as co-authoring a number of articles with Professor Ellis on Central Australian Aboriginal music.

**Catherine Berndt** (BA, Univ. of N.Z., MA, Dip.Anthrop., Sydney; PhD, London: Hon.D. Litt., Univ. of W.A.) is an Honorary Research Fellow in the Department of Anthropology, University of Western Australia. She was born in New Zealand (one of her great-great-grandmothers was a Maori). In Sydney she met and later married a fellow student, with whom she carried out field research in Aboriginal Australia and in the New Guinea Highlands. Together and separately they have published widely in these fields. Her special focus is on women's perspectives. She is a foundation member of the Australian Institute of Aboriginal Studies, a Fellow of the Academy of Social Sciences in Australia, and an Honorary Fellow of the Royal Anthropological Institute.

**Peggy Brock** is Historian with the Aboriginal Heritage Branch of the Department of Environment and Planning in South Australia. She has researched and written histories of various Aboriginal communities in South Australia including the Adnjamathanha of the north Flinders Ranges and Poonindie Mission on Eyre Peninsula. She is the author of two books and various articles on Aboriginal history.

**Catherine Ellis** has worked on Australian Aboriginal music for over 30 years, and is the author of numerous publications in the fields of Aboriginal music and music education, including her recent book *Aboriginal Music: Education for Living. Cross-cultural Experience from South Australia* (St Lucia: University of Queensland Press, 1985). She helped to set up the Centre for Aboriginal Studies in Music at the University of Adelaide, and is currently the Head of the Department of Music at the University of New England, Armidale.

**Fay Gale** is Professor of Geography at the University of Adelaide. Whilst Aboriginal people from northern Australia had been periodic visitors to her parents' home, she was first introduced to Aboriginal women in southern South Australia in 1949 when she stayed on her aunt's property near the Point McLeay Mission. After completing an Honours degree in Geography at the University of Adelaide she became a teacher, and later returned to the University as a PhD student to undertake a study of Aboriginal people moving out of the segregated reserves of South Australia into the integrated social conditions of towns and cities. Professor Gale took some years off to raise a family but, during this time, she retained social contact with Aboriginal friends and her foster sisters. In 1966 she took up a position of Lecturer at the University of Adelaide and was appointed Professor there in 1978. All of her research has concentrated upon the social conditions of Aboriginal people through studies of poverty and women. Her current work deals with the injustices faced by young Aboriginal offenders.

**Jen Gibson** is a mother, trained anthropologist and teacher. She has worked with Aboriginal people in Bass Strait, Tasmania, and in Roebourne and Kalumburu, Western Australia, and has tutored at the University of W.A. She taught and lectured in Montessori education. From 1985 to 1987 she recorded oral history for the Oodnadatta Aboriginal community, South Australia. She is currently a research scholar with the Australian Institute of Aboriginal Studies, working in the Marree region of South Australia.

**Luise Hercus** is a linguist in the Faculty of Asian Studies at the Australian National University. She has been working with Aboriginal people and recording their languages for the past 26 years. She is presently preparing a grammar of the Wangkangurru–Arabana language of north-east South Australia and has worked with these and neighbouring peoples for many years, visiting and recording mythological sites in the region.

**Jane Jacobs** has done postgraduate research on the politics of Aboriginal land rights in Port Augusta and the issue of changing concepts of place as they relate to the political environment. She has co-authored a book on the conservation of cultural heritage sites in Australia and is a PhD student at London University College.

**Helen Payne** is an ethnomusicologist whose research interest is Aboriginal women's ritual life, particularly the musical aspects of it, as practised around the Musgrave Ranges. Her publications have emphasised the interconnection between women's rites and sites in this area. As part of her current work as a lecturer in Aboriginal Studies at the South Australian College of Advanced Education she is assisting and encouraging Aboriginal women to write their own accounts of what it means to be an Aboriginal woman.

# INTRODUCTION

## Peggy Brock

THIS BOOK grew out of a report to the Aboriginal Heritage Branch of the Department of Environment and Planning in South Australia. The report aimed to inform and influence government policy and practice in relation to Aboriginal women. It is important that not only public servants, but also the general public, should be made aware of the issues relating to women in Aboriginal societies. It is to this end that the book has been collated. The following chapters, except the final one by Fay Gale, are based on the reports commissioned by the Aboriginal Heritage Branch from researchers who have extensive experience working with Aboriginal women in South Australia. The authors agreed to rewrite their reports for publication, and Professor Gale has contributed a chapter on southern South Australia to give the book a regional balance.

The contributors are all women who have worked with Aboriginal people in South Australia over a period covering 47 years. Although their accumulated research does not include all communities and areas of South Australia, it does cover a wide range of Aboriginal experience. The authors come from a variety of disciplines, hence the variety in the way they perceive Aboriginal society and in what they look for when undertaking their research. They have been careful to maintain the trust they have established with the people, and where possible have referred their contributions back to the women who have authority over the knowledge they discuss (this has not been possible where information was gathered many years ago). Nevertheless the opinions expressed are their own and do not necessarily reflect either the views of the Aboriginal people with whom they worked or of the Department of Environment and Planning.

**Catherine Berndt**, who undertook detailed research with a range of Aboriginal communities in South Australia in the 1940s, discusses the results of her research at Ooldea in the far west, Oodnadatta in the far north, and the lower Murray River area. She uses her knowledge of these varied communities to show that, despite this diversity, generalisations can be made about Aboriginal experiences since the advent of non-Aboriginal people on their lands. She points out that while the lines of transmission of cultural knowledge have changed, this does not invalidate present-day knowledge. She also discusses the range and variety of female cultural authority and the role of women in these communities. She discusses a trend in some areas, including the Western Desert, for women to lose ground in their involvement in religious affairs.

**Catherine Ellis** and **Linda Barwick** base their chapter on field work carried out by Ellis in the 1960s and early 1970s with Antikirinja women at Indulkana and other areas in northern South Australia. They discuss the extensive cultural knowledge that the women reveal through music and song, a cultural life for the most part maintained separately from the men's ceremonial life. They show how this public separation of cultural activity is not strictly maintained, however, as there is evidence that many female and male ceremonies are similar and that at one time a ceremony may be regarded as men-only and at another time as open or women-only.

**Helen Payne** has also worked with women in the north-west of South Australia. Her observations, based on research with Pitjantjatjara women at Ernabella, complement Ellis' and Barwick's chapter. She discusses the relationship between women's rites and associated sites and analyses what sites are and how they are maintained physically and spiritually. She concludes there is no fixed immutable relationship between women, rites and sites, emphasising the flexibility and adaptibility of Aboriginal ceremonial life.

Moving further south we come to Oodnadatta, an Aboriginal community with whom **Jen Gibson** has worked over the past three years. The Aboriginal community she observed has changed markedly from the people Berndt lived with in the 1940s. Oodnadatta is now largely an Aboriginal town, since the north–south railway line has by-passed the town and the railway workers have moved away. Much of the traditional cultural activity and knowledge, however, has given way to a lifestyle increasingly influenced by western culture. Gibson documents the women's knowledge and their status in their own community.

Port Augusta, at the head of Spencer Gulf, attracts Aboriginal

people from all over South Australia and particularly from the
north and west. **Jane Jacobs** has worked with many of the women
in the town over the past eight years, and particularly with the
Adnjamathanha from the Flinders Ranges and the Kukata from
north and west of the town. She finds that the traditional methods
of passing on cultural knowledge have broken down among these
people and that those with knowledge suffer anxiety and concern
about the most appropriate way of communicating and protecting
their culture.

**Luise Hercus** has also encountered this breakdown in communication of cultural knowledge in the Lake Eyre basin in the north-
east of the State. She has worked with people in the region since
the mid-1960s. She analyses the factors that have resulted in the
undermining of traditional Aboriginal culture in the area and how
this has affected the status of women's cultural knowledge. She also
compares the relatively open shared ceremonial knowledge and
activity of the people of the Lake Eyre region with the more closed
gender divisions of the Western Desert people and the impact of
Western Desert culture on the Lake Eyre basin.

**Fay Gale** reconstructs the status of Aboriginal women in the
cultures of southern South Australia from documentary evidence
and her own first-hand knowledge of people from Point McLeay
on Lake Alexandrina, whom she first met in 1949. She concludes
that women have always been figures of authority and repositories
of cultural knowledge among the Ngarrenjeri and this authority
continues to be exercised by the women today.

This volume is more than an anthology of essays on a common
theme. It sets out deliberately to challenge a number of widespread
preconceptions about Aboriginal society and its interaction with
the wider non-Aboriginal society of Australia. It builds on recent
scholarship that has drastically modified the view of Aboriginal
women propagated by 19th and early 20th century reports, which
described them as drudges and slaves. It seemed apparent to these
earlier observers (with a few exceptions, see Gale's chapter) that as
Aboriginal women worked hard, they worked for the men and
under their direction and were therefore their slaves. These
observers unconsciously based their assessments on their knowledge of their own society; they could not conceive of women
undertaking autonomous economic activity. They also assumed
that women were sexually exploited because they were married
young, without their consent, often before or at puberty, to older
polygamous men. They did not investigate, as have some recent
researchers, what the function of the young wife was in the family
economic unit, but assumed her role was purely sexual.

These observations were made by men (and some women) who were necessarily imposing their cultural values on Aboriginal society. Those who observed and wrote about Aborigines tended to be interested in Aboriginal society either because it was exotic, in which case they concentrated on the most dramatic aspects of the culture, or because they believed they had a mission to save the Aborigines from a life of which they deeply disapproved. In both cases, they were recording what they chose to see. Many expected to find 'primitive', 'stone age' people who mistreated their women, who were guided by superstitions and who led a brutal ritual life; not surprisingly, that is what they saw. The evangelists recorded the 'immoral' life from which they wanted to save the Aborigines, while the ethnologists documented the peculiarities of 'primitive' life. Most of these chroniclers were men, who dealt primarily with Aboriginal men. Their perceptions of a male predominance in Aboriginal society were reinforced by Aboriginal custom, which allowed men to reveal only to other specified men that knowledge for which they as men were personally responsible. The chroniclers were also swayed by the fact that, in white society, all political and religious power was in the male domain.

These attitudes have resulted in certain aspects of Aboriginal cultural life being researched to the neglect or misinterpretation of others. Two examples of this gender bias emerge from my own study of the Adnjamathanha of the north Flinders Ranges, and other peoples of north-eastern South Australia. There has been a longstanding preoccupation among anthropologists with Aboriginal initiation ceremonies, a preoccupation that has blinded them to other aspects of Aboriginal life. There has also been a commonly held assumption that the female roles of wife and mother carry as little power and authority in Aboriginal society as they do in western society.

## Non-Aboriginal attitudes to initiation ceremonies

Male initiation is a dramatic ceremony which has caught the attention of many ethnologists and anthropologists and is generally presented by them as the pivotal event in the Aboriginal life cycle. As such the ceremony takes on a significance of its own, out of context with the rest of life. The field notes of C. P. Mountford (Mountford–Sheard Collection, State Library of South Australia), for example, on the Adnjamathanha people of the Flinders Ranges, concentrated heavily on the initiation ceremonies, the mythology and the rock art. Mountford recorded in great detail the initiation ceremonies he witnessed. By the time he encountered the Adnjamathanha these ceremonies were in a sense one of the last bastions of traditional ceremonial activity to hold out against the onslaught of western influence. Mountford devoted disproportionate amounts of time and effort to recording all aspects of initiation, while its context in the life cycle of an Adnjamathanha man and his society was not investigated in detail. For instance, Mountford supplies no documentation of early boyhood, or the life of men after initiation and their roles in society. Nor does he explain why some men were given more responsibility in the community than others.

On one visit to Nepabunna, the mission where most Adnjamathanha lived at the time, Mountford was accompanied by a young female co-worker, Alison Harvey. She collected information from the women and the results were published in an article (Mountford and Harvey, 1941) covering conception, pregnancy, birth, marriage, menstruation, puberty ceremonies and care of children.

Despite the brevity of this research trip and the lack of access to authoritative female knowledge, this article describes more phases in the female life cycle than Mountford recorded of the male life cycle in any of his various trips to study the Adnjamathanha. He failed to consider that any one event in a woman's life might be imbued with a significance comparable to that of male initiation. Instead, Mountford interpreted the woman's role purely in terms of her physiological function. This despite the fact that it must have been evident to him that some of the older women, from whom he gained information on a variety of subjects, were very powerful figures in the community. The Mountford and Harvey article does not consider any religious, ceremonial or political roles the women may have played in Adnjamathanha life.

Norman Tindale is another male anthropologist who privileged the initiation ceremony over any other cultural and religious activity (Tindale, 1974). His map of Aboriginal Australia divides tribal groups into three great cultural blocs. The first comprises people who practised circumcision, the second people who practised circumcision and subincision, and the third people who did not practise either technique when initiating boys. He does not explain why these particular activities during initiation ceremonies are the major factors which mark one cultural group from another. Tindale takes it as self-evident that male initiation is the central ceremonial and religious event in Aboriginal life and therefore different methods of initiating boys must indicate vital cultural differences among Aboriginal peoples. It is possible that this observation tells us more about the sensitivities of European males than about Aboriginal society.

The categorisation of areas of Aboriginal Australia in the fashion espoused by Tindale raises several problems. First, it is virtually impossible to reconstruct a hypothetical past for Aboriginal people from materials collected up to a century and a half after first contact with Europeans (Tindale started his research in the 1920s and is still working). Tindale was attempting the impossible when he wrote that he:

> endeavoured to give a clear picture of the distributions of all aboriginal tribes as they were prior to the onset of major disruptions and displacements that have accompanied the coming of Western man during the nineteenth and early twentieth century (Tindale, 1974: 5)

While Tindale has much valuable material, it is 20th century information projected back onto the 19th and late 18th centuries, and even earlier (though not pre-contact), documentary evidence; it does not represent a single point in time.

Second, there is much evidence to indicate that Aboriginal society was never static, but was always adapting and changing (see chapters by Ellis and Barwick, and Payne). It is, therefore, misleading to indicate, as Tindale does, that specific ritual behaviour, such as incision practices, was always contained within strictly defined geographic areas.

Third, and most important to the current argument, Tindale ignores all other cultural, religious and linguistic activities. The line he draws to delineate the easternmost limit of the subincision rite (that is the division between those peoples who subincise and circumcise and those who only circumcise) starts north of Port Broughton on Yorke Peninsula, runs through Hawker and the middle of the Flinders Ranges and continues north between Lakes Gregory and Blanche into the Northern Territory. This line runs right through the territory of a tribal group not recognised by Tindale, the Adnjamathanha of the Flinders Ranges. If incision practices divided peoples as dramatically as Tindale suggests, the Adnjamathanha could not exist. Although it is not possible to determine whether the Adnjamathanha always existed as a separate entity, or whether they are only a recent amalgam of several peoples, they claim ancestors on both sides of Tindale's subincision line. Today the Adnjamathanha trace their descent from the Kuyani and Wailpi on the western side of Tindale's line and the Yadliyawara and Pirlatapa on the eastern side of the line. How were these people able to undertake joint ceremonies and intermarry if they came from such dramatically different cultural blocs?

Another example of how Tindale's incision line appears to

divide people with common cultural bonds is found in Luise Hercus' contribution to this book. She sets out another categorisation of the cultural/linguistic groups of north-eastern South Australia. She claims:

> People belonging to the same subgroup were closely connected and their languages were mutually comprehensible
> . . . All the people in the area [that is Lake Eyre basin] even those belonging to different language groups were, however, linked by their joint traditions and their similar social structure. (p. 60).

Tindale's subincising line runs through the middle of Hercus' subgroup, the Karna: the Pirlatapa, Yandruwantha and Yawarawarrka were to the east of the line and Diyari, Thirrari and Ngamini to the west, dividing peoples with similar languages and traditions.

How important is the ceremony which indicates that a boy has become a man and the method used to symbolise this transition? Does it override all other factors in determining Aboriginal cultural affiliations? It is apparent that there are many other factors including language, mythological dreaming tracks, trade routes and reciprocal marriage arrangements which need to be considered before cultural blocs can be definitively identified.

The over-emphasis that Mountford, Tindale and other researchers give to initiation ceremonies stems from their preoccupation with male authority and their ignorance of female economic and religious activity. Most of these researchers were, in fact, not in a position to investigate female roles in any depth because they did not have access to authoritative, female knowledge. The Berndts, whose field work started in the early 1940s, were better placed as a husband and wife team to gain access to information many contemporary anthropologists lacked or ignored. Their detailed study of the Ooldea region, researched and written in the early 1940s, is an example of a balanced interpretation of the male and female dynamics of Aboriginal life (R. and C. Berndt, 1945).

### Undervaluing female roles

Female anthropologists, reacting against previous male bias, have tended to measure female knowledge and power against male authority, so that Aboriginal gender relations are viewed as 'a see-saw balanced on a central fulcrum with women sitting on one end and men on the other' (Hamilton, 1981a: 74). Hamilton has suggested that a more realistic way of describing Aboriginal society is that it 'appear[s] to show both acute sexual inequalities and a high level of autonomy for women' (Hamilton, 1981a: 85). This view of Aboriginal society eliminates the problem of having to compare men's and women's roles and allows one to assess them in their own, often separate, spheres of influence. It enables an assessment of purely female activities without relegating them to a secondary role just because they are female.

One of the more obvious areas of female involvement is procreation and childbirth. In western society, control of these activities is not considered a basis of power within society, thus much of the literature on Aboriginal procreation has also down-graded its importance. Aboriginal attitudes to paternity, pregnancy and childbirth differ from attitudes in societies where paternal inheritance is a major avenue to power and prestige.

Throughout much of Aboriginal Australia it was believed that procreation was determined not only by the impregnation of a woman by a man, but also through other mystical intervention. This was often seen by western observers as an indication that Aborigines did not understand the physiological basis of repro-duction, but it may just be that they considered it irrelevant (see R. and C. Berndt, 1945; Hamilton, 1981). In many Aboriginal communities, people's responsibilities for the land and their totemic associations are determined by where the mother becomes aware she is pregnant; in other communities these affiliations are determined by a person's birth place. Both these locations can to a degree be determined by the mother. In some societies it is a male relative who 'dreams' the child and its paternity or totemic affiliation, but again this 'dreaming' must be associated with a pregnancy, so the mother has a measure of unacknowledged control over when and how this occurs as she determines when the pregnancy is publicly acknowledged.

Among the Adnjamathanha it was believed that children origin-ated from two mythical sky women, each representing one of the two matrilineal moieties. Spirit children swarmed over their breasts and gained sustenance from them. These spirits descended to the ground and when a suitable woman came near, a spirit child would enter under the thumb nail, travel up the arm and into the womb (Mountford and Harvey, 1941: 166–67). The father was not associated with the conception of the child (Mountford and Harvey, 1941: 159). The Berndts suggest this was true of many of the matrilineal descent groups in South Australia (R. and C. Berndt, 1945). The woman, therefore, was culturally acknowl-edged as being in control of the timing of conception (that is, of the time at which her pregnancy is publicly acknowledged), and also of the birth place of the child with its associated responsibilities. Together with the principle of matrilineal descent, this apparent control of conception was to serve the Adnjamathanha well after Europeans moved on to their lands and interbred. A child was deemed to be Adnjamathanha through its mother, so any child of mixed descent born to an Adnjamathanha woman was accepted as Adnjamathanha, and the husband of the mother brought the child up as his own. This may help explain why the Adnjamathanha have survived so well in post-contact times, where neighbouring peoples have dispersed or disappeared.

It is, therefore, dangerous to attribute the same value to motherhood among Aboriginal peoples as has been historically assigned to it for western women. Aboriginal women had greater control over their own bodies and their children's inherited rights because acknowledged social paternity was not necessarily associated with physical paternity. Western women have seldom been in a position to control any aspects of conception and birth (see P. Crawford, 1983: 63–70).

It is important for the future of Aboriginal women that past views of their status and cultural roles are reviewed and revised, because in the past 10 to 15 years a new issue has emerged to complicate the already complex question of knowledge and authority in Aboriginal society. That issue is rights to land, as set out not in Aboriginal law, but in legislation and conservation practice. An Aboriginal person, who has rights to land and can speak for the land, has authority both in Aboriginal and white society, and ultimately perhaps some economic return. So, at a time when researchers are acknowledging the full extent of women's knowledge and power in Aboriginal society, the judicial system and the bureaucracy are dealing with Aboriginal men over rights to land. This has often been done with the connivance of the men, who are acquiring from their non-Aboriginal counterparts the conviction that control of land should belong to men. This attitude is further undermining the status of women throughout Aboriginal Australia, by bringing into question their land-based knowledge (see Jacobs' chapters).

Diane Bell points out that if men alone are consulted over rights to land, women are left without legal status or experience in negotiation. Referring to her own experiences in the Northern Territory, she states:

... the preparation, hearing and recommendations of a land claim have lasting ramifications. A list of traditional owners is produced. This can be varied, but experience has been shown that this is done to limit rather than expand. Women may thus never be entered as traditional owners . . . does it matter? It does, in that the persons with the status of statutory traditional owners are the persons who are consulted in matters of resource management. (Bell, 1984–85: 361)

The research presented in this book indicates that it is not always a simple task to ascertain who has rights to land, because of the complex cultural changes of the past century and a half. The position of women should be assessed in relation to these changes. Information collected today may differ from information gathered 50 years or even 20 years ago, because some knowledge has remained more relevant to present lifestyles than other knowledge, or because knowledge has been deliberately discarded, in the absence of appropriate people to whom it may be transmitted. Movement of people away from their traditional lands and high death rates among Aborigines have contributed to this. Nevertheless, Aboriginal women's status and rights should not be overlooked and they should be encouraged to defend them, as they have done in the past.

**References**

Bell, D. (1984–85) 'Aboriginal Women and Land: Learning from The Northern Territory Experience' *Anthropological Forum* 5, 3 pp. 353–63

Berndt, R. and C. (1942–1945) 'A Preliminary report of field work in the Ooldea region, western South Australia' *Oceania* 12, 4; 13, 1–4; 14, 1–4; 15, 1–2

Berndt, C.H. (1984–85) 'Women's Place . . .' *Anthropological Forum* 5, 3, pp. 347–52

Brock, P. (1985) *Yura and Udnyu. A History of the Adnyamathanha of the North Flinders Ranges* Adelaide: Wakefield Press

Colishaw, G. (1978) 'Infanticide in Aboriginal Australia' *Oceania* 48, 4

Hamilton, A. (1977) 'Aboriginal Women: The means of production' in J. Mercer (ed.) *The Other Half. Women in Australian Society* Victoria: Penguin Books

—— (1981) *Nature and Nurture. Aboriginal Child-rearing in north central Arnhem Land* Canberra: Australian Institute of Aboriginal Studies

—— (1981) 'A Complex Strategical Situation: Gender and Power in Aboriginal Australia' in N. Grieve and P. Grimshaw (eds) *Australian Women. Feminist Perspectives* Melbourne: Oxford University Press, pp. 69–85

Mountford, C.P. Fieldnotes, Flinders Ranges, 19 and 20, Mountford-Sheard Collection, State Library of South Australia

Mountford, C.P. and Harvey, A. (1941) 'Women of the Adnjamatana tribe of the Northern Flinders Ranges, South Australia' *Oceania* 12

Ryan, L. (1986) 'Aboriginal Women and Agency in the process of con-
    quest: a review of some recent work' *Australian Feminist Studies* 2
Tindale, N.B. (1974) *Aboriginal Tribes of Australia. Their Terrain, Environ-
    mental Controls, Distribution, Limits and Proper Names* Canberra: Austra-
    lian National University Press
Tunbridge, D. (1988) *Flinders Ranges Dreaming* Canberra: Aboriginal
    Studies Press

# 1

# RETROSPECT, AND PROSPECT
## Looking back over 50 years

### Catherine H. Berndt

PEOPLE ALWAYS use the past selectively, whether it is their own past or someone else's. Even reasonably well substantiated 'facts' can never be seen in their total context, and 'the whole truth' is an elusive and largely relative concept. Interpretations and re-interpretations are inevitable, in written as well as orally and graphically transmitted material. Continuities, dislocations, changing emphases, even definition of such terms as 'tradition, traditional', belong within this dimension. So does the question of knowledge, or information, about the past.

## Questions

The issues noted here have specific reference to South Australia, and to Aboriginal people, but they are also of more general concern: what women know about mythological and historic sites, and related matters, in contrast to what men know; how the situation has changed through time; how to explore these questions; and how to avoid or redress a gender imbalance in this respect. The problems (and they *are* problems) are much less simple than they appear on the surface.

1

When I began to prepare this chapter I intended to keep it fairly impersonal, drawing on data derived from fieldwork experiences without spelling out research procedures. This is not the place for an account of research designs and techniques. Nevertheless, the 'how' aspect of research is directly relevant. Not least, it is about 'who' in relation to 'what': who is asking, who is being asked, what are the questions? Who is witnessing or participating in (or excluded from) what, when and where, in what circumstances? And so on.

Such questions have provided an indispensable framework in all the field research I have been involved in over the years. One major emphasis, however, was present from the very beginning (in 1941). Ooldea was my first experience with Aboriginal people. My husband was with me and we worked as a wife–husband team, but our perspectives were different. He concentrated on men, I concentrated on women. This was an acceptable and approved division of labour in Aboriginal communities where gender distinctions were conventionally defined. In that respect I was conforming with the local rules. Later, in some areas (in the Wave Hill camp in the Northern Territory, for instance), as a stranger I was at first invited to attend men-only ritual performances, or hear men-only songs and other verbal material. I invariably declined. Aligning myself with women was not only regarded by women (and men) as the proper thing to do, it also gave me a better insight into women's views on everyday and religious affairs, including the kinds of unspoken or not-publicly-expressed knowledge shared by men and women as a basis of collaboration or interdependence between them.

**Times and places**

The places I turn to now are Ooldea, near the Transcontinental Railway Line, in 1941; the lower River Murray, including Point McLeay and Murray Bridge in the early 1940s, along with Adelaide city and a number of country towns; and Oodnadatta and adjacent areas in 1944.

*Ooldea*

Ooldea siding, on the railway line between Adelaide (via Port Pirie) and Perth, was in 1941 home to a few fettlers and gangers and their families, a watering halt for steam engines, an optional stop for travellers on the main passenger trains, and a supply-stop for the weekly tea-and-sugar train. About four miles north of the line, on flat ground among the sandhills, was Yuldi Gabi, Ooldea Water or Ooldea 'Soak', where the United Aborigines Mission had established a small settlement in 1933. In 1941 the mission was working not only to 'protect' Aboriginal people from the kinds of contact they were experiencing with non-Aborigines along the line and to convert them to Christianity, but also to abolish traditional Aboriginal culture, generally, and in that particular area. However, the missionaries were not at first openly antagonistic to our research. They had cooperated in 1939 with the Board for Anthropological Research of the University of Adelaide, in an expedition of which my husband had been a member.

We did not want to locate our field base at the mission station, and the missionaries seemed to be opposed to our living in the Aboriginal camp. In any case, the camp was fairly mobile, moving at intervals to make fresh windbreaks and shelters on the sandy slopes and hollows above the soak. We finally chose a clearing half way down to it, beside the track that people usually used in coming and going to get water or to visit the mission station for rations or work. Mostly they would pause at our camp, so that apart from the time we spent with them in their own camp setting, we were able to meet most of them in that way too.

The Aboriginal population at Ooldea was mobile in another sense, not only in camping arrangements. People came and went along the railway line. Some had come originally from farther west — from Karonie and Laverton, for instance. From time to time little groups emerged from the 'spinifex country' to the north, toward the central ranges. When columns of smoke appeared on the northern horizon, moving closer, missionaries would hurry to send out clothing so that the newcomers would not arrive naked at the soak. This influx of people speaking no English and bringing their own ceremonies and religious rites was exciting in a different sense to the local people. In their struggle to find and keep a foothold in the European-dominated situation, they were in the process of losing or submerging much of their traditional knowledge and activities. The new arrivals were like a breath of fresh air, a re-vitalizing force, enhancing their awareness of their own Aboriginal identity. The differences between them were a source of discussion and comment, but almost insignificant in comparison with the differences between all of them on one hand, and non-Aborigines on the other.

People on their way to and from the soak gathered to watch as we pitched our tents and arranged our windbreaks and open fire, and several of them joined in to arrange the branches and get buckets of water. After that we settled down to learn how to 'hear and understand and talk properly' with them. A shifting assortment of women helped me, along with a few 'regulars', in what was at first a rather difficult task for all of us. It improved gradually, as I tried to build up a sizeable vocabulary, and women taught me short songs and stories along with conversational material. They were patient and friendly, but in the beginning the process seemed painfully slow.

As regards sites, some of the stories that were told to me, especially in the first few weeks, included no place names at all. When I asked about these, the answer was that the events had happened 'out spinifex' and had no specific locations—or if they had, the story-teller didn't know them. As I came to know the women better (and *vice versa*), and to be less dependent on English in simple discussions and translations, I realised that there could be other reasons as well. In regard to *mamu*, for instance, malignant spirit-characters, many stories and many ordinary comments dealt with *mamu* in general: they could be anywhere and everywhere. Adults as well as children were warned to beware of potential dangers in various shapes: apparently harmless stone spear-heads lying in the sand (strong winds that changed the contours of the more exposed sandhills used to uncover hundreds of these blades); or strangers who could not easily be identified; or seemingly familiar persons, even close relatives. They might be *mamu* in disguise. Virtually all *mamu* were believed to be hostile to human beings, even when they pretended to be friendly. Nevertheless, some were of the Dreaming, inhabitants of the land from the Beginning; and in *their* case, site names were built into their stories—with two provisos: the names could be omitted if the story-teller insisted that she was ignorant, or if she thought that it would be too hard to explain to me where the site was located or that I would not really be interested. That applied also to other stories.

In the last couple of months, I noticed that more *djugurba/tjukurpa* (Dreaming) stories and discussions were forthcoming without any pressure on my part. Among them were 'star' stories and other material which women had previously remarked, in passing, were men's business. Site names were more likely to be attached to stories of this kind. Also, aside from the camp ceremonies, and other ritual proceedings, women offered to show me dances that were not to be seen by men.

When we first arrived at Ooldea there were about 200 people in the main camp. A few weeks later, following heavy rains that they expected would fill the waterholes in the 'spinifex country' to the north and north-west, all but about 80 of them set off in that direction. Then the numbers began to build up again as groups gathered at Ooldea for the ceremonial season at new-moon time in August. Participants came from the west and along the railway line as well as from the north, until there were between 400 and 500. Small ceremonies and less elaborate ritual affairs had been going on at intervals, on other occasions, but this large-scale complex of activities was very different indeed. In one dimension, at the level of interpersonal relations, it allowed plenty of scope for informal discussions and plans, exchange of news and gossip—and the passing on of topical information about sites and resources as well as about the whereabouts of other people. At another, it afforded entertainment in the shape of ordinary ceremonies and songs. And, above all, there was the organising of the various aspects of the central *raison d'être* of the whole assembly—the religious rituals, and the supporting arrangements (such as supply of food and other necessities) that made them possible.

For everyone there, not only for myself, this concentrated mixture of scenes provided opportunities to engage in discussions about people and places and events; to affirm or re-assert their own knowledge and expertise; or (for younger people or those from other areas, for instance) to learn more about any or all of these things, including the rules governing partial or total prohibitions and exclusions. I was able to see and to hear what women did and said, separately or in conjunction with men, and to compare this with what they had been telling me. Of course, a great deal escaped me, especially in regard to finer points but also in regard to the complex field of meanings and interpretations. At least I was not the only one in that position, nor the only young woman who was a 'learner' with a long way to go in the process of understanding. That applied to most if not all young women, even to those who were better equipped to take full advantage of that process in their local setting.

Two things were quite clear, in everyday affairs but even more prominently in the ceremonial and ritual context. First: women handled their roles, their part in such activities, with authority and confidence: they knew what they were doing and what they should be doing, and how all this fitted in with what men were doing. They acknowledged conceptually a realm of what could be designated 'men's business' as contrasted with 'women's business', and a fluctuating intermediate zone where these two overlapped.

Second: the women who acted with authority and articulate directions were mostly middle-aged, not old enough to be physically incapacitated nor so young as to be ill-equipped for such responsibility. They knew how to balance their own authority against men's, and how to deal with the more conspicuous and vocal dominance sometimes displayed by men. I did not realise that at first, just as I did not realise what I later interpreted as 'independent interdependence' in overall interrelations between men and women. The discrepancies between what I was told at first (e.g. 'Only men talk about the stars!') and what I was told later were rather like a verbal screen, adjusted to cope with ignorant enquirers—or, in some cases, ignorant or not very well informed respondents.

We were at Ooldea for a little over six months. If we had been in a position to stay longer, even for only another six months, and I had been able to become more fluent, I am sure that *my* knowledge of women's knowledge would have accelerated and expanded at an increasing rate. This was plain when later, on a short visit to the Warburton Range area in Western Australia, I was introduced to women's song sequences and rites on the basis of what I already knew and could talk about with them. It was especially evident at Balgo, also in Western Australia, on the edge of the Great Sandy Desert, where the vocabulary I had acquired at Ooldea was useful among Gugadja and Mandjildjara speakers, as were other features of 'Ooldea Desert culture'. In research there between early in 1958 and late in 1985, I paid particular attention to women's associations with land (as well as to women's rituals), the 'land maps' they carried in their heads, and the myths and songs that were, they believed, inseparable from the actual sites. With a longer period at Ooldea I am reasonably sure I could have done almost the same there—notwithstanding what even at that time seemed to be the imminent destruction of much of the local Aboriginal heritage.

*Oodnadatta; Macumba*

Oodnadatta in 1944 was a small town in northern South Australia, on the railway line between Port Augusta and Alice Springs. Some women of partly Aboriginal physical descent and partly Aboriginal cultural upbringing lived in the town, but the main Aboriginal camp was a short distance away. We stayed at the unpretentious little pub in the town, because at that time we were trying to explore relations between Aboriginal and non-Aboriginal people. We were also examining written documents, such as police records, at Oodnadatta as well as in Port Augusta and other country towns. We visited Ernabella and various station properties on the way there, and later camped near Macumba station to participate in an initiation sequence. The people involved in the initiation activities included men, women and children from a wide range of pastoral stations. Not everyone from the town camp took part, but most had some share in the overall proceedings and some links with those who did. There was an air of effervescence, almost a 'holiday' atmosphere (especially for the station people), alongside the serious and emotionally intense ritual component that provided the explicit reason for it all.

Again, I concentrated on working with women. Although I did not record a great deal in the way of myths and songs, it was obvious that women were well informed about their territorial linkages, and their own place in religious matters. When they covered their heads on ritual occasions, in their own camps, or while their husbands were welcomed with a penis-holding rite, this was simply polite behaviour and not a sign of 'exclusion'.

Three quotations are relevant to this area, and to the main theme, in different ways, although none of them refer directly to sites.

The first (R.M. and C.H. Berndt 1951: 183–5) is from a short account of a two-part semi-sacred ceremony with mixed Aranda and Antingari elements, part of a preliminary sequence leading to the initiation ritual that was to follow a few weeks later.

Just before sunset, nearly all the men, women and children gathered at the Antingari camp. The men clustered in a circle about one large fire, and near them the women and children were gathered around three smaller fires. Then the songs began.

The men beat on the ground, in unison, with boomerangs and short sticks. Women clapped their thighs with both hands together, keeping time to the rhythm and making a sonorous background to the singing. Middle-aged and older women took a prominent part, helping to decide the order in which the songs should be sung, and sometimes altering the pitch of their voices to sing in harmony. . .

A new song was started up, and women and children lay down and pulled blankets over their heads, while the men kept on singing . . . Then suddenly the women and children lifted their heads; they flung aside their blankets, and stretched out their right hands, with a long-drawn 'Ahhh!' towards a figure that came dancing into the light. [The tall headdress worn by this dancer was a thread-cross] *a wanigi* or *waniga*, which among the Antingari, southern Aranda and Pidjandjara people is usually shown only in the sacred or totemic rituals that initiated men perform [in men-only contexts, although rather similar headdresses were worn in public ceremonies at Ooldea. After an interval for supper in

the various family camps, voices came calling from one camp
to another that the second performance was about to start].
This time, after the women and children had hidden their
faces (and then uncovered them), five dancing-men came
stepping into the firelight. . .

The main points here are the role played by 'middle-aged and
older women'; women's responsibility for ensuring that their own
and their children's heads were covered so that they did not see
particular sections of the men's dancing, although they could hear
the songs quite clearly; and their awareness of the exact stage at
which they should hide, and later uncover, their heads. (I did not
know the songs, and had to rely on following their lead.) This part
of the procedure has close counterparts in other places (eg. in the
Laverton area of Western Australia), and was not regarded as an
unjust imposition or a sign of subordination, but as a dramatic
diversion that added to the excitement of the occasion.
    The second quotation (C.H. Berndt, 1965: 277) takes up one of
the points just noted. A series of men's initiation rites was in
process in a secluded area of a station property (Macumba) at a
little distance from Oodnadatta. At intervals, women and children
moved away from the main camp, leaving it free for men-only
concerns.

    One man, occasionally two, armed with spears and
thrower, kept the women's camp constantly under
surveillance; ostensibly for protection against any danger,
but also to make sure that no-one strayed in the wrong
direction. One evening, the women had made camp as usual
in the sandy bed of a dry creek and we were settling down for
the night; then, in the stillness, we heard plainly the sound
of the men's singing. At once, there was feverish activity.
Picking up our little bundles of firewood, our firesticks, and
what we could carry of the leafy boughs of our windbreaks, we
struggled higher up the creekbed in the half light, the
'guardian' moving parallel and almost out of sight. Presently
the leaders among the women decided we had gone far
enough: we built up the fires again, arranged the windbreaks,
and prepared to sleep. But once more, as the talk and bustle
died down, the sound of men's singing came clearly, though
more faintly, on the wind. This time the leaders sat up, and
looked at one another with what can only be called silent
exasperation. A bitterly cold wind was blowing down the
creekbed, everyone was tired after a long day, and it was clear
that nobody wanted to move again. With no word spoken
and, as far as I could see, no hand-signs, first one and then the
others began to sing. They kept this up, just loudly enough

to blot out the rise and fall of the men's voices, until either the wind changed or the men stopped singing. The women paused, and listened: when they were sure that all was quite, they curled up on the sand by their fires and went to sleep.

This case, and others like it, suggest that women were very ready to fall in with the men's demands: but that they sometimes did so in their own way, not strictly according to instructions. They were prepared to keep up appearances: in effect 'The men don't want us to hear them singing, so we'll make sure that we don't.' Collusion is too strong a word, but we can certainly speak of collaboration. [I added (p. 277) that] it is possible to build up a picture, not only of 'what women know', but also of their attitudes toward this ritual division of labour and the ordering of their own behaviour in relation to it—including agreement on what *need* not be said.

I come back to this point later. The third quotation illustrates a negative view of women's place in Aboriginal religious affairs, and a mistaken assumption. The last sentence in it refers to the initiation sequence at Macumba already mentioned.

Maddock, I wrote (C.H. Berndt, 1981: 189):

denigrates women's place in religious affairs. Women and men are, in this respect, he says, separated by a great chasm, and that separation is ritually dramatised. He quotes Elkin, and virtually goes beyond Elkin, in outlining and interpreting the Jabuduruwa (Yabuduruwa) sequence (Maddock 1972: 147–9; italics in original) in which, he suggests, 'women have penetrated the secret area without looking at the secret things before their eyes. Despite being so *close* to secret things, they are as *far* as ever from knowledge of them.' He has already put this as, 'Were the women to look they would see ... sights forbidden to them. It is possible of course that they are dazzled' by the flames springing up as they walk around the ritual ground, using cylindrical bark emblems to beat the fire there. Note that he does not say, 'They did not see', or 'could not see', but implies that they would not or could not. This is a dubious assumption. (From my personal experience of a comparable though not ritually identical event, I know that other female participants as well as myself were able to, and did, glimpse a great deal of what went on beyond the firelight.)

The women who were helping me to understand what was going on at Macumba had already alerted me to that part of the sequence. To summarise:

We all move towards the place where the men are gathered behind a line of fires. When we get close to them we see 'something' coming from the darkness on the other side of the fires, coming towards us. We all turn around and run back, while the men throw burning firesticks over our heads · · ·

They did not describe or specify what we would see; but the painted and decorated novices riding astride men's shoulders were very clearly visible as we turned to run, among the brilliant sparks from the firesticks and the echoing shouts and singing. It was an excitingly dramatic occasion, exhilarating for the women as well as for the men. It was also an example of the interdependence between men and women that was a salient feature of traditional Aboriginal religious life.

## Lower River Murray, Point McLeay, Adelaide city

Our research in these places had two facets: in one we focused on what the Aboriginal people considered to be distinctively Aboriginal and coming from a distinctively Aboriginal past, 'nothing to do with Europeans, only Aboriginal.' Of course this was an idealised image, hard to define except when it was linked with localised territorial and language names. The general label 'Aboriginal culture' is no substitute for these, and can imply loss or absence of *local* cultural continuity.

The area we covered together in the early 1940s included Point McLeay, Murray Bridge, Tailem Bend, Meningie and Wellington on the lower Murray, and several country towns north-west of Adelaide—Walleroo, Maitland and Port Victoria (near Point Pearce). (My husband had begun his association with his main friend and teacher and adoptive 'father', Albert Karloan, in 1939.) We were on inter-visiting terms with a range of people of Aboriginal descent in Adelaide; we camped for several months at Murray Bridge reserve to be near Albert Karloan, and were identified as Aboriginal people by tourists and curious locals who wanted to see 'how the Abos lived'; and after Albert died, we were allowed to camp in the shearing shed at Brinkley Station, to be near Pinkie Mack and her family at the Brinkley Native Reserve. We also went through documents and records whenever these were available, with permission to hunt through old papers and record books. Many of these, except in the case of Point McLeay, were in metal bins and boxes in outdoor sheds; some were badly damaged, in one place shredded by nesting mice. We were told in a number of places that even the more intact papers, especially the oldest, were about to be handed over to the paper-salvage collectors. (Later we heard that some, at Port Augusta, had been accidentally destroyed by fire.)

A fairly detailed coverage of both perspectives ('traditional' and 'changing') in this region is contained in our manuscript volume (R.M. and C.H. Berndt, n.d.). The range of people's interest in their Aboriginal past extended from those who showed some concern with what they saw as their local Aboriginal heritage, to others who had 'passed' or were trying to 'pass' into the wider society. The only persons who still had a relatively thorough knowledge of their traditional cultures were Albert Karloan and Pinkie Mack. There was a certain amount of friendly rivalry between them; but this was not on the basis of gender, because the traditional culture of the region was remarkable in at least one respect (among others). Gender-based differences in the sense of inclusion–exclusion, in religious and other affairs, were minimal. The nearest parallel in this respect was/is the Tiwi culture of Bathurst and Melville Islands. Karloan was the last living Yaraldi man to have gone through the full initiation sequence. Pinkie's had been a version of the less elaborate sequence for girls, which was abandoned before the boys' initiation was; however, Pinkie knew the main details of it. She had been born in the bush; and she went through a modified initiation ritual of having clan marks put on her chest and shoulders.

Point McLeay mission station was established in 1859 by the Reverend George Taplin, and had a profound influence on the lower Murray and Lakes region. Taplin's attitude to Aboriginal culture was made up of two dimensions, over and above his humane concern for Aborigines as people. He was interested in studying Aboriginal culture, putting it on record in so far as he could achieve that. Nevertheless he did his best to destroy it as a *living* culture. Its place, as he saw it, was in the past, surviving only in written accounts of what had been done there before it was replaced by Christianity. He did not, apparently, envisage the possibility that such accounts could be a source of information for Aboriginal people who might want to use them for any sort of cultural revival. Certainly the combined effects of mission teaching, liquor, loss of land and food resources, introduced diseases and the influx of Europeans were devastating, not only in regard to people's activities but also in disrupting the transmission of knowledge between adults and children.

Albert Karloan was born at Point McLeay in 1864 and went to school there for a time. His father was a famous Aboriginal doctor, a healer; and his father's sister was notorious for her sorcery skills and knowledge, some of which she taught Albert when he was a boy. Pinkie Mack, 73 years old when we first met her, obtained much of her traditional knowledge from her mother Louisa

Karpeny—who, according to the mission records, was 100 years old when she died in 1921. Pinkie was a notable singer, or song-woman: not that she usually composed songs herself, but she remembered a great many. (Among the few she could not recall were some of the girls' initiation songs.) However, she married 'up the River', and a great deal of her cultural knowledge and personal experiences lay outside the lower Murray area. Nevertheless, when she returned to that area it was obvious that she knew more about its past than did virtually all of the people who had continued to live there; and after Albert's death she was the main authority, or the main repository, to whom people could turn for information about that past—and about the relationships between them in the present. Even though her memory was beginning to fail in some re-spects, she was always active, lively and ready for a discussion, preferably in regard to matters of Aboriginal culture in the areas she knew personally. On one occasion when she was visiting Adelaide, and travelling in a tram with two other elderly Abori-ginal women (and myself), she embarrassed them by telling one of them, loudly and jovially, 'What you want is a man!' She added, to me, 'That's our custom. The thing to do is to marry a young man! It keeps you young!'

One of the features of traditional culture most often cited by women as well as men was sorcery, including the names of several varieties, and some of the details. They were mentioned especially in times of stress—for example, when someone was complaining about being unjustly treated by government officials, or particular-ly by the Aborigines Protection Board. Also, in sociable gatherings in people's homes of an evening (or at the home of my husband's father, where we stayed when we were in Adelaide), if Pinkie Mack was present, sooner or later she would start to sing, and encourage others to join in—and not only 'Point McLeay people', because 'mixed marriages' had brought some Point McLeay and Point Pearce families together in Adelaide city. Otherwise, most conver-sations dwelt on the problems and pleasures and the on-going business of living in a situation dominated by people of non-Aboriginal descent. In Adelaide and in country towns and along the lower River Murray, women in widely different circumstances made such remarks as, 'We're like white people now—nobody tells us who we've got to marry, we can please ourselves'; and, 'We're civilised, not like those people up north!' Or, 'I can't speak my own language, only English!'

Adelaide was one focus for individual visitors and for families wanting to settle in a city away from what they thought was the less tolerant atmosphere in country towns. It was a mixing ground for people whose Aboriginal backgrounds were quite diverse. As against that, Point Pearce and Point McLeay were centres with a long-standing core of inhabitants who had a history of common residence and common experience. Even persons who were officially barred from living in such communities because they had been 'exempted' from the provisions of 'the Act' could keep in touch with those who continued to live there.

Just to look at the lower Murray situation, the population that was often referred to by the general name of 'Point McLeay people' is an especially interesting case. It is true that detailed knowledge of traditional Aboriginal culture was almost lost, and that their culture no longer survived as a living force. The local languages were no longer the main media of communication, marriage rules no longer applied, almost everything of the Aboriginal past seemed to have gone. The face of the landscape had changed, and the signs of European occupation were visible almost everywhere. But the Point McLeay mission had one positive advantage. It was located strategically in a richly fertile natural environment, and not overshadowed or crowded-in by a congestion of other settlements. Above all, it provided a central focus for a population which had continuity of occupation over a long period. 'Point McLeay people' visiting Adelaide tended to keep their own identity, as at least a nominal point of orientation. Children growing up in or around Point McLeay or in places along the River were able to get acquainted with basic information about topography, resources and events that adults already knew: where whales could be expected to come in, at what seasons—and so on; and who had lived or died or was buried, or what had happened at which places.

The people were not divorced from their country: the country itself was there, a visible and tangible sign of the long perspective they could draw upon in underlining their relationship with it. In the early 1940s both men and women, voicing their discontent with the restrictions and disadvantages they were experiencing, often raised the issue of their prior ownership of the land: not so much in terms of specific sites, but in terms of the larger, overall expanse of the country, the region that was special to them. This intermeshing of locality and ideas about locality continues to be a significant factor, which in one sense overrides or transcends the dimension of detailed site knowledge. A region represents to them an overall collection of sites that has its own emotional and identity-marking and economic ties with the distinctively Aboriginal past.

**Questions, Answers?**

It is very difficult to assess the amount and quality of women's knowledge in comparison with men's, without having information on the total range. The issue of relative age and ritual status points to differential 'knowledge' within gender divisions, and a further contrast hinges on what might be called passive knowledge as against active expression—in verbal or ritual actions, for example. Aside from questions of secrecy, Aboriginal women have been called an almost invisible population in regard to major religious affairs. Their contributions and their very real authority are more easily overlooked than the more obtrusive and spectacular and often more large-scale affairs that are visibly controlled by men.

Because Aboriginal women have been accorded such a negative role in religious and even in everyday matters, as contrasted with men, this bias appears to have influenced some current Aboriginal views—particularly, Aboriginal *men's* views. And it is not only male writers who have taken this negative approach. Women writers as different in many respects as Daisy Bates and I.M. White have virtually aligned themselves on the same negative side of the fence in this regard. I.M. White's (1970) assertion that Aboriginal men and women are 'partners' loses its force when she qualifies it by arguing that women are merely 'junior partners'. She adds (1975; 140) that women regard men in their religious manifestation with 'extreme reverence and respect'. (Her main field research areas were in South Australia.) In other instances there can be statements that are unintentionally misleading. For example, we have sometimes used the expression 'men's rituals' for ritual sequences arranged or dominated by men, even when these were said to be intended for the benefit of the community or group as a whole and not (or not explicitly) for their own. We prefer now to use the label 'men-only' for this aspect of 'men's business'.

On the opposite side of the fence are the contrasting claims that insist on the superiority of women and 'play down' the prestige of men. In her Northern Territory studies, Diane Bell emphasises the positive role of women in traditional Aboriginal life, including religious affairs. Among other things, she sees women as the main nurturers of land, implying that men have a lesser responsibility in caring ritually for sites, especially important sites. This stance is just as biased as are statements that favour the 'inferiority' of women; but it does not seem to have been as effective in influencing public—and Aboriginal—opinion. In some places, including Western Desert areas impinging on and extending into South Australia, women actually seem to have lost ground, where men assert their own dominance in religious affairs.

While cause-and-effect claims are hard to substantiate, the influence of non-Aboriginal views about the status of men *vis-à-vis* women in public life, including authority in the religious sphere, does seem to have played a part here. And this has obvious implications for current perspectives on 'country' and associated matters, especially where differences of opinion occur regarding 'who knows best'. (Even in eastern Arnhem Land, a region of the Northern Territory where there had been a trend toward greater 'openness' and flexibility in religious affairs, and a long-standing recognition of the significance of women in that respect, a contrary trend is also becoming entrenched. One man now prominent as a painter, for instance, assured me dogmatically, in mid-1988, that women in that region had nothing to which the various terms for 'sacred' could be applied: in effect, they were outside the sphere of religion, or merely on its fringes.) This kind of issue was, and is, less salient in regard to the lower River Murray people, whose traditional culture did not impose such dilemmas on them— whereas in other regions a division of labour that was workable and dramatically useful before, has become less so in the face of concerted pressures from outside.

On the topic of Aboriginal women's cultural knowledge as compared with men's, not nearly enough has been done in regard to documenting and recording and assembling more than a fraction of the relevant information. Women themselves, of course, would have been in the best position to compile detailed accounts on this score, along with interpretations and commentaries. Being members of a non-literate society can have disadvantages as well as benefits: they had no means of putting such material on record in any durable way. Moreover, because in their traditional past they were concentrating on their own cultural perspectives, their own regional cultures, their comparative range of interest and enquiry extended only so far. And then there is the factor of what should not be said, or written, publicly even though 'everyone knows it'; or should be only hinted at, or mentioned obliquely and within a certain range of people. This area of unspoken or partly verbalised understanding is an integral part of the whole complex. In my own enquiries, beginning at Ooldea in 1941, my impression is that I have been personally involved in a slow process of learning which is still a long way from completed, if it ever could be. It is certainly a more complex picture of cross-cutting linkages, obligations and responsibilities than a sharper male–female contrast would imply.

Because so much could be said on these topics, I note a few of what I see as some of the main issues, without elaborating.

One is the question of defining the term 'Aboriginal' in this connection. As it stands now, it appears as a homogeneous category with no internal distinctions. That is all very well for certain purposes: but how does it mesh with the subject of 'cultural knowledge'? We come back here to the question of 'Who . . .?' This question was crucial in traditional Aboriginal contexts. 'Who knows what?' Or, 'doesn't know, or shouldn't know?' And so on. 'How does he or she know? Who told/showed her?' At Ooldea I did not realise, as I did later, the importance of such questions. Later I would ask, after hearing a story (for example), 'Who told you?' or 'Where did you first hear that?' (Or, 'see that'.) In enquiring about 'cultural knowledge' now, these questions are even more important, and likely to become still more so. Reading and tape and videotape material, interchange of ideas on 'cultural' topics through deliberate teaching and informal personal contacts: these and other factors are producing a cultural blend which has no similar precedent, and which impinges on 'information' associated with local sites and territories as well. Remember that in sacred matters there could be secrecy between groups and categories of women, or of men, even in one community, or one region.

Traditionally, the main lines of transmission within a community were (in a sense) vertical, a teaching-and-learning process from one generation to another. There were peer-group influences too, of course. 'Lateral' influences from other Aboriginal communities were a vehicle for innovation and change, but internal checks and sanctions sometimes seem to have kept them within limits. Now, these no longer apply.

In seeking information about 'cultural knowledge' in these circumstances, it is of course, not enough to choose 'an Aboriginal person' or 'a woman'. That is likely to be a surface or band-aid measure, defeating the purpose of such an enquiry.

Second, the 'Point McLeay case' does not invalidate the argument that information about sites and country generally is a crucial factor. In the call for 'land rights', or *recognition* of land rights, land is a visible, tangible ingredient. In many cases there is a possibility of negotiation and even of restoration. Information, or knowledge, relating to such land is not so easily restored, and in many cases it is irretrievable. That applies less in regions where Aborigines have been able to sustain continuity in cultural transmission, but uncertainties are increasing in those circumstances too.

Third, information about sites needs to include also information about 'tracks' going through or near them: not only, 'Who is there?' but 'Who went past, going which way?' And so on. That applies especially to *sacred* sites. For *secret*-sacred sites the questions need to be framed more cautiously—paying even more attention to the 'who' framework. Sites of direct or indirect, past or present ritual/mythic significance, sites that are or were tabu or restricted, closed to men or to women, need to be tackled carefully.

But 'sites of significance' is a more general category. It includes other areas of concern but without religious overtones. At one level the associations may be immediately-past or even fairly distant-in-time human beings, close relatives or others, perhaps reported by name. At another level they are remembered as scenes of events that took place in the human past, but not linked with known or individually identified persons: the scene of a fight, for instance, or a burial. (But in the Great Victoria Desert, after a final burial-rite graves were not accorded special consideration and were simply absorbed into the landscape.)

A new kind of 'sites of significance' has been developing in the recent past. To some people of Aboriginal descent who were not reared in a living–traditional Aboriginal culture, almost everything of that culture which they hear about or read about now is, by definition, sacred, or almost so. And that applies to 'country' as well: all sites in Australia are 'sites of significance' because they are, or were, *Aboriginal* sites.

Fourth, if people can't get information about their own local past beyond the memory of living, or recently living persons, because the lines of transmission have been broken or blocked, what can they do?

Perhaps they can say, as some have already done in such circumstances, 'As of *now*, this is how it is—or was. This is how it could have been, or might have been.' In the present trend towards a generalised Aboriginal culture with 'islands' of local–cultural survival, this is a likely outcome. The current efforts of the Heritage Branch in South Australia are not quite too late to explore these 'islands' and their changing contexts.

The situations outlined here, different in many respects, are fundamentally very similar. In all of them, people of Aboriginal descent were dominated in varying ways and to varying degrees by people of non-Aboriginal descent who occupied the main positions of authority—and power. That applied also in circumstances where Aborigines felt they still had a measure of relative independence, as in the matter of ceremonial and ritual arrangements in the Ooldea and Oodnadatta areas. Even then, they were limited in the range of decisions they could make, and their movements across the country were mostly subject to pressures outside Aboriginal control. In the central Reserves and in the 'spinifex country' they were less conscious of this, but Europeans were beginning to encroach on these areas too, in the shape of missionaries, police, pastoralists, prospectors, and other travellers. Once they ventured into the zones of closer European settlement, even on the peripheries, Aborigines were 'caught': they were drawn into the new system (new for them) and unable or partly unwilling to escape from it.

Ooldea in 1941 was like a microcosm where traditional Aboriginal elements were coming into sharp contact, and often conflict, with foreign elements that the people concerned found hard to interpret. The waves of Aboriginal newcomers from the north strengthened the Aboriginal side, but that could go only so far. At the same time, they were helping in the process of developing a broader-than-local awareness of Aboriginal identity. And in that process Aborigines were able to make use of some of the unfamiliar resources they found in the mixed array of materials and services that confronted them. The less imposing manifestations of the transcontinental train, especially the open goods-wagons, were convenient vehicles, travel-aids, for individual persons and groups on religious or mundane journeys. They could move eastward or westward, on short or long journeys, sustaining or enlarging their network of relations with other Aboriginal people and their information on other Aboriginal places and affairs.

Oodnadatta too was a mixing-ground, not only for people of Aboriginal descent and European and other non-Aborigines who were focused on the town, but also for so-called 'bush people' whose centre of interest was their own Aboriginal world. Ernabella at that time was a mission station, but with a more self-consciously liberal and tolerant approach than many others, such as the United Aborigines Mission. Missionaries and police and pastoral station people discouraged the eastward movement of Aborigines from that area, but the impact of Western Desert culture was far from negligible. However, in the circumstances there were limits to that too.

As for Adelaide city, Aboriginal people from other areas, not merely from the lower River Murray and Point Pearce, had been coming and going for some time on a fairly small scale. People from the middle north, from the Lake Eyre basin, from Port Augusta and beyond, were visiting or already living there. To some extent this was influencing, for example, the Point McLeay orientation or the core 'Narrinyeri-ness' of the lower River Murray people. But it was widening the social-heritage perspective of Aboriginal people, even though that perspective was held in check at that time by the formidable pressures of official and unofficial assimilation policies.

So, the situations we have been looking at do not present a picture of the past, as something that is over and done with. They are a telescopic survey of the diminution or dilution of traditional Aboriginal culture (as it was in the era of independent Aboriginal control of their own affairs), and a change to a pan-Aboriginal perspective or orientation that is still trying to find appropriate niches for specific local continuities. The transition is a difficult one, but the focus on land is a potential medium for reconciliation between local and wider concerns, as well as a basis for discussion of such issues as the preservation or sustaining of knowledge about the Aboriginal past-in-the-present.

## References

Bell, D. (1983) *Daughters of the Dreaming* Melbourne: McPhee Gribble/ George Allen and Unwin

Berndt, C.H. (1965) 'Women and the "secret life" ' in R.M. and C.H. Berndt (eds) *Aboriginal Man in Australia* Sydney: Angus and Robertson, pp. 238–82

—— (1970) 'Digging sticks and spears, or, the two-sex model' in F. Gale (ed.) *Woman's Role in Aboriginal Society* Canberra: Australian Institute of Aboriginal Studies, pp. 39–48 (1974, 1978, 1986 editions, pp. 64–84)

—— (1981) 'Interpretations and "facts" in Aboriginal Australia' in F. Dahlberg (ed.) *Woman the Gatherer* New Haven and London: Yale University Press, pp. 153–203

—— (1984–85) 'Women's place ...' *Anthropological Forum* 5, 3, pp. 347–52

—— (1988) 'Phyllis Mary Kaberry' in U. Gacs et al. (eds) *Women Anthro-* (see especially pp. 169–70)

Berndt, R.M. and C.H. (1945, 1942–45) *A Preliminary Report of Fieldwork in the Ooldea region, western South Australia* Oceania Bound Offprint Sydney: Australian National Research Council, pp. 1–343

—— (1951–52) *From Black to White in South Australia* Melbourne: Cheshire, Chicago: University of Chicago Press

—— (n.d.) 'A World That Was ... (Manuscript on Yaraldi people of the lower River Murray, South Australia; with the Wakefield Press, Adelaide)

Gale, F. (1972) *Urban Aborigines* Canberra: Australian National University Press

Kaberry, P. (1939) *Aboriginal Woman: Sacred and Profane* London: Routledge

Maddock, K. (1972) *The Australian Aborigines. A portrait of their society* London: Allen Lane/Penguin (Revised edition 1982)

Taplin, G. ed. (1879) *The Folklore, Manners and Customs of the South Australian Aborigines* Adelaide: Government Printer (Johnson Reprint 1967)

White, I.M. (1970) 'Aboriginal women's status: a paradox resolved' in
    F. Gale (ed.) *Woman's Role in Aboriginal Society* Canberra: Australian
    Institute of Aboriginal Studies, pp 36–49
—— (1975) 'Sexual conquest and submission in the myths of central Aus-
    tralia' in L.R. Hiatt (ed.) *Australian Aboriginal Mythology* Canberra:
    Australian Institute of Aboriginal Studies, pp 123–42

# 2

# ANTIKIRINJA WOMEN'S SONG KNOWLEDGE 1963–72
## *Its significance in Antikirinja culture*

Catherine J. Ellis and Linda Barwick

WE WILL be drawing here on the fieldwork done with Aboriginal women performers by Catherine Ellis in the north of South Australia in the period 1963 to 1972. This outline of the information gathered at that time and the attendent difficulties of collection may be useful in three ways: to contribute to an overall picture of women's knowledge in this area, to give an historical perspective on the present-day situation, and as a guide to prospective field workers, for many of the same problems for field workers will still be applicable.

One of the most important points that must be understood about traditional cultural knowledge in Central Australia is that it is centred on song knowledge. The definition of a knowledgeable person is the person 'knowing many songs', for without song knowledge, information about places, laws, correct behaviour, healing, food sources and a host of other items is unavailable. In the eastern Western Desert, as in other parts of Central Australia, rights to land and relationship to country are articulated in the performance of song series or songlines relating to the travels of the Ancestral Beings through the country in the Dreaming times.

Each ceremonial performance is made up of a number of verses or small songs (*inma tjukutjuku*). Present-day performers are believed to tap the power of their Dreaming ancestors by presentation of the appropriate melodies, texts and rhythms, designs and dances for each small song, which relates to the activities of the ancestor either at a particular named site, or while the principal character was travelling through a particular stretch of country. The performance of the correct sequence of small songs constitutes a map of the ancestor's journey, and mythological significance is often attributed to the particular geological formations present at the sites, which came to assume their present-day form as a result of actions of the ancestors in the Dreaming.

Because Ellis's fieldwork was mainly concerned with documenting the musical features of these songs, the information presented in this report draws extensively on data gathered at the time of performances of the secret women's ceremonies central to Antikirinja culture. The body of women's cultural knowledge centred around these ceremonies ranges from practical knowledge of the habitat and use of plant and animal species; to intimate acquaintance with the country being ritually celebrated, and the ways in which individuals are related to land through ritual and kinship affiliations; to more esoteric understanding of the power of the Dreaming and how to draw upon it in order to control the women's physical and social environments.

**Relevant literature**

The area on which Ellis's field work concentrated was the eastern Western Desert. The performers with whom she worked most closely identified themselves as Antikirinja and Pitjantjatjara speakers. Apart from the work done by Ellis and her collaborators, which will be dealt with in detail in another section, the major researchers to have dealt with women's cultural knowledge in this area are Annette Hamilton, an anthropologist who has published a number of articles based on her fieldwork at Everard Park (now Mimili) in 1970–1 (Hamilton, 1980, 1981, 1982), and Helen Payne, an ethnomusicologist whose work on women's ceremonies has involved fieldwork at a number of places in the north-west of South Australia, including Pukatja (formerly Ernabella; see Payne, 1984). The anthropologists Isobel White (1974, 1977) and Catherine Berndt (1974) have also published material based on fieldwork in this and contiguous areas of the Western Desert cultural group, as has the ethnomusicologist Margaret Kartomi (1984).

Luise Hercus, with whom Ellis worked on various occasions, has concentrated more on eastern South Australia, especially on the Arabana and Wangkangurru people, the easterly neighbours of the Antikirinja speakers (see Hercus's contribution in the present collection). Material from other areas that is of general relevance to the question of Aboriginal women's cultural knowledge may be found in the works of Diane Bell (1983), Fay Gale (1974, 1983), Gillian Cowlishaw (1982), Jennifer Green (1981), Barbara Glow-czewski (1981), and Nancy Munn (1973).

## History of fieldwork

The first recordings of Antikirinja women's secret singing were made by Ellis at Port Augusta in 1963, on the insistence of knowledgeable men who knew the importance of having a woman collector record women's songs (cf. Hamilton, 1980:16). Initially, because the women were so shy, one of the men came out to the ceremonial ground with them to encourage them to sing, but before the end of the first day's recording the women were enjoying the experience and prepared to perform songs that no men were allowed to hear. Thereafter, Ellis found no difficulty with women's willingness to perform, it being only necessary for her to explain to women she had not previously met what had already been sung, or to carry greetings from one singer to another. In conjunction with the linguist Luise Hercus, Ellis recorded more Antikirinja women's songs in 1965 and 1966.

By this time Ellis had become aware that the women's ceremonial material was more complex than any one researcher could handle from the base of a single subject discipline. During a performance there was always much more going on than one person was capable of noting, recording or filming. It was also becoming very clear that the women's secret knowledge would not survive indefinitely, as many of the singers were old women who had not taught their descendants in the normal way. It was therefore decided to set up a group project to carry out intensive fieldwork on Antikirinja women's ceremonies.

The resulting Group Project on Andagarinja (Antikirinja) women was financed by the Australian Institute of Aboriginal Studies, the University of Adelaide, Monash University and the Board for Anthropological Research (S.A.), as well as by the members of the expedition themselves. The members of the first expedition in September 1966 were Rhonda Buckley (photo-grapher), Catherine Ellis (leader and ethnomusicologist), Luise Hercus (linguist), Lynda Penny (social psychologist) and Isobel

White (anthropologist). The team recorded women's material in Marree and Oodnadatta, and the results were published in a private publication (Buckley et al., 1967). The second group expedition, undertaken in May 1967, consisted of the same personnel with the exception of Lynda Penny. This group recorded material in Marree, Oodnadatta, Indulkana Creek (where most of the work was done), Coober Pedy and Port Augusta (Buckley et al., 1968). A third group expedition returning to Indulkana, Coober Pedy and Port Augusta was undertaken in 1968 by the same personnel, but the results never reached a final publishable form.

These three expeditions documented numerous Antikirinja women's ceremonies, recording them in the following forms:
1 taped recordings of music, language and song explanations;
2 written song texts, genealogies, maps and drawings related to the ceremonies;
3 photographs (both black and white prints and coloured slides) and film footage.

In subsequent years, Ellis recorded more material from the same women, most often at Port Augusta and in the Indulkana area. Relevant material in Ellis' field collection was recorded in 1969 at Oodnadatta, Port Augusta, Indulkana and contiguous areas, Anna Creek, Hamilton, Macumba Station, and Copper Hills, and in 1972 in Port Augusta. Map 2.1 shows the locations of the places in which the material was recorded.

## Discussion

There are eight main women's ceremonies documented in Ellis's field collection, but not all performers were familiar with all songs. These ceremonies referred to sites ranging from Fowler's Bay and Port Augusta in the south to Hermannsburg, Papunya and Alice Springs in the north (see Map 2.1). Most ceremonies related to songlines traversing quite large tracts of country, but one was particularly devoted to a single important ceremonial site at Indulkana, and this was the only performance to have been recorded near the actual site celebrated in the song. Although the site in question was only a few kilometres away, the performers apparently felt no pressing need to perform the song at the actual location. It is possible that the researchers' interest in recording the songs wherever they happened to come across the performers may have led to a greater than usual proportion of ceremonies

**Map 2.1    The extent of Ellis' research with Antikirinja women**

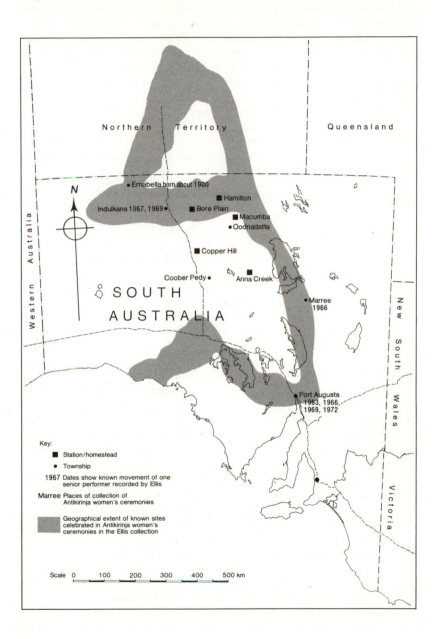

being performed away from the sites celebrated, but it is nevertheless clear from this and other examples that it was not unusual
for performances to occur away from the sites celebrated.

Nevertheless, our evidence suggests that the women had quite
detailed knowledge of sites. Although many of the sites celebrated
in the women's ceremonies were neither in traditional Antikirinja
country nor in the country in which the performers were currently
resident, they had extensive knowledge of the sites and their
sequence, and drew a number of maps showing the routes covered
by the ancestral journeys. The lack of details on the locations of a
number of the recorded performances appears to be due to our
failure to elicit this information at the time of recording rather
than to the performers' ignorance.

The presence in the women's repertoire of ceremonies relating
to places outside of traditional Antikirinja country may be related
to the fact that several of the senior Antikirinja women had been
born in places that had formerly been Arrernte or Arabana
country, because their parents had migrated to these areas.
Although contact with Europeans and the pastoral industry
indubitably played a major part in these population movements, it
is now clear that Western Desert cultural practices had been far
from static even before the contact era (see Hamilton, 1982). It
seems possible that rights conferred by birth in what was formerly
Arrernte country may be part of the reason for the Antikirinja
women having so many Arrernte songs in their repertoire, even
though they did not understand the language. This may be
particularly so when the ancestor concerned had also passed
through the Antikirinja country of the woman's parents, through
whom she may have inherited additional rights to that line.

At least one of the senior Antikirinja women appears to fit this
pattern; her parents came from Ernabella, but she was born at a
site on the Finke River in Arrernte territory that was an important
Arrernte site for one of the Antikirinja women's ceremonies,
which she told the research team was her 'Dreaming'. The
ancestral characters involved had also passed through the Ernabella region, where her family returned after her birth. She played
a leading part in a number of performances of this ceremony used
for healing purposes, although she was not the principle owner.
She also appeared to have some special rights in relation to the
performance of another portion of the same ceremony purchased
from outside the Antikirinja area, despite the fact that she knew
neither the language of the texts nor the explanations for this
portion.

Few of the Antikirinja women recorded in this sample were still living in what had traditionally been their ritual country. Many had moved for work or to live in their husband's country. It is unclear to what extent this is a continuation of traditional practices in which women were usually married to men from a different country, and would often have lived away from their birthplaces in their husbands' country.

Helen Payne (1984:277) notes that at the time of her fieldwork with Pitjantjatjara women in the 1970s most women had relatively fixed residence in the country of their husbands, although these women were starting to push to return to their own Dreaming country to enforce their ritual rights. Because of limitations on access to vehicles that would enable them to visit relevant sites away from the current place of residence (men could not be involved in the staging of women's secret ceremonies), some of the women with whom Payne worked were being challenged over their rights to ceremonies related to these sites by women of other communities located nearer to the sites. On the other hand, ceremonies located in the country to which the same women had moved were performed without challenge despite the lack of inherited rights to the ceremonies. Payne argues that knowledge of the country gained by long residence was a factor that interacted with inherited rights to the relevant ceremonies in determining the actual state of claims to ownership. (Note that Payne's data on Pitjantjatjara women at Pukatja indicates that ceremonial performance at the relevant sites was much more common than we have suggested was usually the case with Antikirinja women's ceremonies. This may be because the Antikirinja women with whom Ellis worked were generally much farther removed from their own country than appears to have been the case for these Pitjantjatjara women.)

Patterns of residence have been determined to some extent by kinship arrangements and totemic affiliations, but these appear never to have been clearcut in the area under discussion, as Annette Hamilton argues persuasively in a number of articles. In a system in which the ideal marriage was between people born in different places on the same totemic line, she argues that a woman's desire to live near her parents in order to share in matrilineally transmitted rights to ceremonies and resources was often in conflict with the desire of her husband to live in and have children born in his own country (Hamilton, 1980:9). We have insufficiently detailed genealogical information on the women performers in our sample to be able to comment on the extent to which our data fits with the model proposed by Hamilton, but what is clear is that there were considerable movements over very wide areas.

An example of the mobility of some of the performers, especially the most senior women, can be given by examining the appearances of just one woman performer in the documentation of the collection. This Antikirinja woman was recorded performing seven of the eight major ceremonies Ellis documented, being the owner of at least three of these (in all of which she danced), while in others she led the singing while the senior owners danced. She was born in the Ernabella area and was related to several of the other senior Antikirinja women. At the time of our fieldwork she came to be officially resident in the old folks' home at Port Augusta, and she was recorded at Port Augusta in 1963, 1966, 1969 and 1972. She had relatives in a number of other places and was also recorded at Marree in 1966 and Indulkana in 1967 and 1969. Map 2.1 shows the relevant places and dates pertaining to this performer.

In general, older women who were senior owners appear to have been more mobile than younger women. As well as trips made for medical treatment or for work purposes, many trips seem to have been made in order to visit female kin. These patterns of movement in the older women may be a larger-scale manifestation of the behaviour observed in the camp by Annette Hamilton: she noted that older women moved at mealtimes from the fire of one daughter to that of another (Hamilton, 1980:12). Hamilton's data also indicates that many women wished to live near their mothers in order to learn their ceremonies (Hamilton, 1980). She cites the cooperative nature of traditional food gathering and, in earlier times, the need to share resources such as the matrilineally inherited but non-transportable grindstones as reasons why women, in conflict with their husbands' wishes, may have tried to live near their parents.

**Performance and transmission of women's songs**

Often the most useful recordings were obtained from women living in the single women's camps at the various places visited; this institution in Central Australia is described in detail by Diane Bell (Bell, 1983). Women in these camps were often separated or widowed, or visiting female relatives in the camp, and secret material could be performed and discussed with no fear of interruption by men, to whom these camps were out of bounds.

The performers generally preferred to present the songs in ceremonial context, although they could be performed in isolation. One particular song series was considered to be too powerful to be performed with all associated painting and dance in full ceremony, so performers decided to present it only in musical form. The song texts appeared to have a number of levels of meaning: an open meaning relating to the ancestor described in the particular song, an erotic meaning relating to the power of the song as love magic, and an esoteric meaning concerning the details of the ancestral myth.

Younger children (boys to about six years and girls to about ten or twelve) were permitted to attend non-secret versions of the ceremonies, and were allowed to know the open meanings of the songs. Some of these songs were allowed to be performed in the hearing of men, and in a few cases open versions were also performed by men as part of a mixed group.

Older girls were permitted to attend ceremonies as learners after the age of about fifteen or sixteen. Only those women who had two or more children were given access to the erotic levels of meaning and could be involved in the secret performances, and when more secret material in the form of healing charms, for instance, was being performed, only the most senior women were involved. Although many of the older women had scarified bodies which may have indicated that they had been through various forms of initiation, these were rarely spoken about. The main criterion for access to secret women's performances was said to be that the performer must have had two children.

It was noticeable that the senior owners of the ceremonies were often those involved in the dancing, while other senior women led the singing. Less knowledgeable performers joined in the singing or simply watched the ceremonies. Even though performance by non-owners was permitted under some circumstances, only the song owners were allowed to give explanations of the song texts; on several occasions performers recorded by Ellis were unable to give explanations because of the absence of the appropriate owners.

Ellis was told that in former times much knowledge had been passed from women to their grand-daughters during the period of isolation at menstruation. With the erosion of this practice of isolation, the whole process of transmission of traditional women's culture was placed in jeopardy. It is worth noting that at the time Ellis was working in the field, children were often being brought up by grandmothers or aunts rather than their biological mothers. In Oodnadatta the mothers of two of the most interested girl children present at the ceremonies did not themselves take part, so that these children were learning from women of their grand-mother's generation. The removal of the frail aged to old folks' homes away from their traditional country also contributes to the breaking down of the traditional education of girls by their maternal grandmothers, in which the sacred songs figure as the central element.

Ellis's work in the field was neither sufficiently intense nor over a sufficiently long period to ascertain the principal modes of inheritance of these ceremonies. It seemed that numerous factors entered into the choice of a new owner, including the woman's conception site along the totemic track of a particular ancestor, as well as inherited rights and assiduity in learning the secret women's repertoire. Certainly these women placed great importance on the secrecy of their sacred rites and the necessity to exclude all men as well as untrustworthy women. Payne (1984) notes that Pitjantjat-jara women at Pukatja in the 1970s inherited secret ceremonies both matrilineally and patrilineally. Hamilton has suggested that matrilineal transmission had been the norm in eastern Western Desert and that a move to patrilineally inherited ceremonial rights is a symptom of men's infiltration of the women's secret life, a process that seems to have been increasing in many areas of northern Central Australia (Hamilton, 1980: 16–17). As evidence she cites Nancy Munn's work with Warlpiri women, which has documented a change over time from matrilineal to patrilineal transmission of women's secret ceremonies (Munn, 1973), al-though more recent work by Diane Bell and Barbara Glowczeski casts some doubt on this.

One well-documented means of transmission of ceremonies was by sale. One ceremony recorded at Oodnadatta had been bought from Alice Springs women by one of the Oodnadatta women, who in turn had subsequently sold the sacred objects associated with it to a group of women later recorded at Coober Pedy. It is not clear whether performance rights had also been sold. The Oodnadatta woman who claimed to have bought the ceremony was able to give very detailed information on the places named in it, which were in the Alice Springs area. Some time later verses of this same series were recorded in Port Augusta. Trading of ceremonies of this kind was apparently well established along the Alice Springs to Port Augusta route.

Another way for new songs to enter the repertoire is through a performer dreaming a new ceremony, in which the ancestor involved will usually teach the associated myth, dance and cere-monial design as well as the song. This may also be the mechanism for 'refinding' a ceremony in the local repertoire that has fallen into temporary disuse when the senior owner has died before being able to pass it on to qualified kin (Payne, 1984: 269). A ceremony performed for Ellis at Indulkana in 1967 was said to have been newly dreamed, but work much later happened to show (quite accidentally) that the same song was known to women in the north of Western Australia. It is unclear whether this was a case of the Indulkana women refinding a song once present in their repertoire, or whether dreaming was a way of incorporating new material possibly learnt when Indulkana women had visited the area involved.

## Relationship of women's and men's repertoires

Annette Hamilton suggests that the existence of women's secret ceremonies complementary to the men's, taken in conjunction with the quite rigid separation of the sexes in day to day activities, means that in this part of Central Australia the two sexes can be described as separate social groups (1981:78; 1980). Hamilton has argued that this rigid separation emphasises the complementarity of women's knowledge to that of the men, and thus enhances women's social power. She comments: '[Women's secret] ceremonies exist as an affirmation of the essentially separate status of women as a group, articulating the spiritual affiliations of women with the Dreaming events often from the same source as the men's, and their rights to exclusivity as women in relation to those events' (Hamilton, 1980:16).

The co-existence of varied forms of the one song line—an open version for men, women and children, a secret men's version and a secret women's version—indicates a high degree of overlap between the forms both sexes maintain are secret. There are a number of reports of the exchange of information between senior women and men on their complementary portions of the one Dreaming (see Hamilton 1981:79), but on all public occasions there was a rigid separation of the sexes in matters of secrecy. In fact, the differences between men's and women's versions usually serve to highlight differences in what may be articulated in front of the other sex. For instance, the sexual exploits of some of the male characters in the women's secret performances would not be presented in the open versions of the same ceremony, although they were the subject of great hilarity in the women's secret performances.

It is clear that throughout Central Australia considerable change has occurred in the ceremonial repertoire of both men and women. For example, Stephen Wild has recently published an article on changes in the repertoire of Warlpiri people at Lajamanu, highlighting 'innovation and adaptation of Warlpiri songs in the light of the history of Lajamanu, Warlpiri relationships to land, taxonomic considerations, the creative process, and Warlpiri relationships with other communities and non-traditional social forces' (Wild, 1987: 97). Because the channels of transmission of men's and women's repertoires are largely independent through-out Central Australia, one might expect that they would have changed in different ways. Annette Hamilton has argued that in the eastern Western Desert 'women continued the older traditions in technology as. . . they continued the older ritual traditions, not because they are innately "conservative" but because innovations in both areas are introduced and elaborated within the context of exclusively male rituals' (Hamilton, 1980:8).

Although our information suggests that a not inconsiderable degree of innovation was in fact taking place in the overall structure of Antikirinja women's repertoire during Ellis's years in the field, it is probably true that the men's repertoire in this area has undergone much more extensive change. Reports indicate that men's ceremonies in the past 20 or 30 years have been developing stronger links with the northern Western Desert region, including an adoption of the subsection system, and this has had a major impact on the men's secret repertoire. For example, the men's ceremonies now include several that are performed at initiation ceremonies by all men, irrespective of their totemic affiliation.

Comparison of the known composition of the women's and the men's repertoires at the time Ellis was working tends to support the suggestion that the women's secret ceremonies belong to an older stage than the men's. For example, in the 1930s and '40s when the first researchers (Tindale, Mountford, the Berndts) were working with Pitjantjatjara and Antikirinja people, one of the women's ceremonies Ellis recorded was an integral part of the men's secret repertoire, but by the time that Ellis was working in the area, only the women appeared to be performing secret versions of it, while open versions were performed by a few men who claimed that this was only a playground corroboree, not a Dreaming. For whatever reasons, this ceremony appears to have dropped out of the men's repertoire but to have been maintained in the women's secret life.

There is usually a musical relationship between women's and men's secret versions of the same Dreaming: in such cases the women's and men's versions may either be different accounts of the same characters, or else they relate to the meeting of two Beings, in which case the men's version will be called by the name of the male being, and the women's version by the name of the female being. However, in the Indulkana area there exist two ceremonies, one an open men's ceremony and one a secret women's ceremony, which have the same species name but which are completely different musically and mythologically. The men's ceremony, in which women may also participate, relates to the travels of that being in country to the west, with Indulkana as the easternmost extent. The women's ceremony relates to the travels of two women of the species from the east towards the country around Ernabella, and is related to other myths collected by Luise Hercus in the Mount Dare area (pers. com.). The differences in the geographical extent of the two myths seems to illustrate a greater tendency of women's ceremonies to relate to the east, while men's tend to relate to the country to the west.

Futhermore, men's and women's ceremonies seem to have some different musical characteristics. Much more research needs to be done in this area, but it seems likely that the men's and women's songlines have different musical norms even though they may be tied through the common performance of open versions.

In a number of cases, men have actually denied the existence of secret women's versions of the same songline, claiming that only the men's version was true and proper (see also Strehlow 1971:392–5). It is for this reason that reports by male anthropologists of the non-existence of women's secret ceremonies in a particular area are not always to be trusted. The women leave the men's views of their knowledge unchallenged most of the time and are prepared to appear subservient to them. However, when major decisions are to be made, or when women's ceremonies are to be presented, the men accept the authority of the senior women. It is clear that in Central Australia these women have held significant power through their particular knowledge of the use of the power of song, a knowledge that is respected by the menfolk and understood as important for the survival of the group.

The concern of many of the women's ceremonies with power over bodies, such as healing and love magic, has been denigrated by some European men as of lesser importance than what have been characterised as the more universal themes of the men's secret ceremonies (see Hamilton 1981:78, citing Maddock 1974:216–17). This judgement derives from that dualism at the heart of western philosophy, involving the spilt between mind and body (and the privileging of the former at the expense of the latter). Thus, in Christian cosmogony, there is a separation of the physical world from the spiritual realm of the Hereafter. By contrast, for Aboriginal Australians the Dreaming has physical as well as non-material power. Therefore, the capacity of women's singing to tap the intangible power of the Dreaming for action upon the bodies of individuals is no less impressive than that invoked by men.

34 *Women, Rites and Sites*

## The power of women's singing

The power of the ancestral being celebrated in the ceremony, released through the simultaneous presentation of the appropriate melody, rhythms, texts, body designs and dance movements, could be used by women for a number of purposes, including love magic, healing, weather control, and control of behaviour. On a more general level women's ceremonies, like the ceremonies of the men, participated in the maintenance of the life energy of the species and the sites being celebrated.

The power of the women's performances was clearly acknowledged by the Indulkana men, who on one occasion approached the research team because they were afraid that the songs the women were performing might cause an elopement. This had just happened in a neighbouring community prior to the team's arrival, and the cause had clearly been identified as the performance by the women of love magic. The women, who knew how successful these performances could be, assured the researchers that the man being 'sung' would see the woman for whom he was sung, no matter how far distant he might be. This process the women called 'singing the eyes' of the chosen partner, and was said to lead to that man coming to the woman for whom he had been sung. This fact was kept secret from the men, partly because of their probable anger.

Although most of the women's secret ceremonies were used for love magic, there were a few used for healing ceremonies, and it was possible to record actual performances of such songs. Richard Moyle (1979:25) notes the use of Pintupi women's love magic songs for healing, although he conjectures a recent change in this direction. Ellis had the impression that both love magic and healing songs were considered to be different uses of the same type of power.

Healing ceremonies could be performed for men or women. At one level they operated to draw the ailing person into the community to experience the support of others in a strong social bonding. At another level, though, these performances were seen as drawing on the power of the song to unlock the life force left in the soil by the ancestor involved. Although such ceremonies should ideally be performed at the site concerned, the song itself was considered to contain sufficient power to change the course of an illness.

One of the healing ceremonies witnessed by Ellis was performed for the husband of one of the singers. He had been ill for some time. Only the most senior women performed this ceremony, which they called 'singing fat'. They took with them to the ceremonial ground the necessary animal fat, and a board on which it was placed. They performed the ceremony over the fat, blowing the song into it, mixing it with their urine, and moistening it when necessary with their saliva. Thus the power of the song, and the power it had generated within the bodies of the women per-formers, was conveyed to the fat, which was subsequently massaged into the ailing man's back. The man himself could not hear the song, only be the recipient of the empowered fat. The performers assured me that the man's health improved dramatically after that performance. (Although most healing songs appeared to be the province of the women, the only song recorded to aid a difficult birth was sung by a man. He explained that he could not be near the woman giving birth, but performed the song within earshot of the women helping her.)

The process of training of performers stressed respect for the power of the ceremonies and for the knowledgeability of the senior performers. The restrictions on access and training functioned to ensure that this power could not be misused by ignorant trainees. The following anecdote illustrates some of the practices and implications of the traditional teaching methods.

One of the most senior women resident at the old folks' home at Port Augusta performed for Ellis a song intended to train young girls. It had been left unperformed for many years, so the singer who led the performance was also instructing the other women present as well as the younger girls for whom the song was intended. The performance consisted of only one small song, which contained the name of the principal character. Initially it was performed solo by the senior singer, and after the first few presentations of it, she began to intone a story (see Ellis, 1983 for a discussion of the musical problem presented in this particular performance). In this way she would tell part of the story, then repeat the small song, after which she would immediately recom-mence intoning the story followed by the next repetition of the song. Gradually the other women present began to join in; those who were older asked the leader some questions which were sometimes answered in discussion outside the actual story telling, sometimes ignored (direct questions were often considered to be ill-mannered). The story that unfolded gradually introduced the principal character whose name occurs in the song. It detailed his actions when he discovered that his young wife had not been faithful to him. The song was regarded as very secret.

The lead singer told us that such songs were regularly taught to young girls and that much of the problem of the behaviour of young people now stemmed from the fact that they were no longer

being taught correct behaviour through constant repetition of the
songs. Such song-learning can be extremely effective as a social
control. The conditioning that occurs on the ceremonial ground,
where the young person is entirely under the domination of the
most senior and most knowledgeable, can easily be invoked
without the need to repeat explicitly secret information, since
humming the melody can encapsulate the meaning for the person
who has been exposed to the full performance.


**Evidence of change over time**

Although the musical system tends to lead to extremely accurate
preservation of the technical details of text, rhythm and melodic
setting in any one item of singing (as is shown by the collection of
the same material in almost identical form over periods of 50 or
more years—see Ellis and Barwick, 1987), the actual sequence of
items in any one performance is much more variable. The ideal of
songs relating to particular sites being performed in a set order is
often referred to by performers, but is not evident in practice;
some variation appears to have been acceptable within traditional
parameters, but it appears likely that at least a proportion of such
deviation is due to the residence of performers away from their
traditional country. Payne points out that the knowledge of the
songs pertaining to sites is most accurate for the sites of greatest
economic significance. Men's and women's knowledge of songs is
important for their orientation in the physical world as well as in
the spiritual world of the ancestors whose lives are recreated
through the songs, and precise details about sites are best pre-
served by people able to maintain contact with the area concerned,
either by residence or visits (Payne, 1984:271).

Undoubtedly one of the factors affecting change in the women's
repertoire has been the changing patterns of life in the areas under
discussion. The place of birth of performers as well as their current
place of residence and the inheritance of rights to songs in the
countries of their parents will all affect the potential pool of songs
in which the performers will be able to participate. It has been
suggested above that the Antikirinja women's knowledge of
Arrernte songs was related to the general eastward movement of
Western Desert peoples into areas of the Centre formerly occupied
by Arrernte-speaking people. We also suggested that the women's
repertoire in the area under discussion may have represented a
more conservative tradition than the men's ceremonial repertoire.

Because of the complex way in which rights to ownership and performance of songs were transmitted, it seems likely that the repertoire of women's songs was always changeable depending on the presence of key performers, although such change appears to have been accelerated by contact with Europeans and European technology. Many of the songs recorded by Ellis had not been performed for many years previously, and some songs known by the performers with whom she worked could not be performed because of physical incapacity of key performers. Performers themselves considered the breakdown of traditional education of performers to be responsible for many social problems as well as the disappearance of numbers of ceremonies.

Another factor affecting performance of certain items in the women's repertoire may be the changing sources of food and women's associated work. For example, with the availability of ready-ground flour, there may no longer be the same need to perform ceremonies for the increase of certain grass-seed species (Knowles and Tunstill, 1983 suggest this to have been the case for men's increase ceremonies in the Indulkana area).

Finally, the desecration of sites and the death of key performers may lead to gaps in the songlines that formerly traversed the continent unbroken. Although it has been reported in a number of cases that the death of key performers has been followed by a redreaming of that ceremony by an appropriately qualified relative (e.g. Payne, 1984:269), it is known that in other cases the lack of suitably qualified descendants (caused by fragmentation of traditional educational practices, disease or genocide) has led to the disappearance of the relevant ceremonies from the repertoire (e.g. Moyle, 1986:45–6).

The individual performer today has a very different set of experiences from her forebears. In many cases the disruption of traditional family structures by the forced removal of children has had devastating effects on the body of women's traditional knowledge, as it has on all traditional culture in these areas. There has also been increasing lack of respect for the senior members of the community and, as has already been mentioned, a breakdown in transmission as a consequence of removing the elderly to old folks' homes in other areas. European education, even when it has been sufficiently enlightened as to include a discussion of some aspects of Aboriginal culture, has tended to downgrade the importance of traditional women's knowledge, and has made the training of young girls, which often took place at the time of seclusion during menstruation, extremely difficult to carry out.

The emphasis given by male anthropologists to the primacy of the men's ceremonial life has probably also affected the political power of women, in that Europeans have assumed that the men are the most important politically and have thus set up consultative processes that tend to exclude women. In part because of this, women have not had the same access as men to money and technical knowledge (especially transport), which has added to the difficulties in maintaining their particular ritual rights and their links to land. Despite this, in some parts of South Australia the women's role was better able than that of the men to survive the fragmentation of traditional culture; indeed, in an urban setting it is the Aboriginal women who have often become the important political leaders.

## Conclusion

This discussion has made clear that Antikirinja women have traditionally played a significant role in traditional culture, possessing a body of knowledge separate from, and complementary to, that of the men. The power released by women's knowledge and performance of sacred ceremonies maintains the life force of the country and the species being celebrated, as well as being available for use for such specific purposes as love magic, healing, and weather control. Because of women's different life patterns we found that their traditional song knowledge in some cases related to quite different areas from those of the men in their communities. In 1963, the Antikirinja women asked Ellis to help them improve their lot through the knowledge she had gained of their songs but, over 25 years, little has been achieved. Their modes of knowledge do not sit well with European institutional practices.

It is of the utmost importance to recognize the real strength and knowledge of Aboriginal women, and to enable them to develop and preserve the song knowledge that they deem essential in the contemporary world. This form of knowledge, which replaces literacy in this society, involves the accurate preservation of information through the careful interlocking of structural elements in the songs, abstract material that cannot be falsely manipulated without the structure of the whole being lost. For Europeans to appreciate this form of knowledge, special training is necessary so that researchers, educators, and knowledgeable Aboriginal women may work together to preserve the unique knowledge and control of the heritage of their people that Aboriginal women possess.

## References

Bell, D. (1983) *Daughters of the Dreaming* Melbourne: McPhee Gribble/ George Allen and Unwin
Berndt, C.H. (1974) 'Digging sticks and spears, or, the two sex model' in F. Gale (ed). *Women's Role in Aboriginal Society* 2nd edn, Canberra: Australian Institute of Aboriginal Studies
Buckley, R., Ellis, C.J., Hercus, L., Penny, L. and White, I.M. (1967) *Group Project on Andagarinja Women* Vol 1, Adelaide: private publication, University of Adelaide Library
Buckley, R., Ellis, C.J., Hercus, L., and White, I.M. (1968) *Group Project on Andagarinja Women* Vol 2, Adelaide: private publication, University of Adelaide Library
Cowlishaw, G. (1982) 'Socialisation and Subordination among Australian Aborigines' *Man* 17, pp. 492–507
Ellis, C.J. (1970) 'The Role of the Ethnomusicologist in the Study of Andagarinja Women's Ceremonies' *Miscellanea Musicologica* 5, pp. 76–209
—— (1983) 'When is a Song Not a Song?' *Bikmaus* 4, 3, pp. 136–44
Ellis, C.J. and Barwick, L.M. (1987) 'Musical Syntax and the Problem of Meaning in a Central Australian Songline' *Musicology Australia* 10, pp. 41–57
Gale, F. ed. (1974) *Women's Role in Aboriginal Society* 2nd edn, Canberra: Australian Institute of Aboriginal Studies
Gale, F. ed. (1983) *We are Bosses Ourselves: The Status and Role of Aboriginal Women Today* Canberra: Australian Institute of Aboriginal Studies
Glowczewski, B. (1981) 'Affaire de Femmes ou Femmes d'Affaires: Les Walpiri du Desert Central Australian' *J. Soc. Ocean* 37, 70–71, pp. 77–91
Green, J. (1981) *Utopia: Women, Country and Batik* Utopia, NT: Utopia Women's Batik Group
Hamilton, A. (1980) 'Dual Social Systems: Technology, Labour and Women's Secret Rites in the eastern Western Desert of Australia' *Oceania* 51, 1, pp. 4–19
—— (1981) 'A Complex Strategical Situtation: Gender and Power in Aboriginal Australia' in N. Grieve and P. Grimshaw (eds) *Australian Women: Feminist Perspectives* Melbourne: Oxford University Press, pp. 69–85
—— (1982) 'Descended from Father, Belonging to Country: Rights to Land in the Australian Western Desert' in E.B. Leacock and R.B. Lee (eds) *Politics and History in Band Societies* Cambridge: Cambridge University Press, pp. 85–108
Kartomi, M. (1984) 'Delineation of Lullaby Style in Three Areas of Aboriginal Australia' in J.C. Kassler and J. Stubington (eds) *Problems and Solutions: Occasional Essays in Musicology presented to Alice M. Moyle* Sydney: Hale & Iremonger, pp. 59–93
Knowles, I. and Tunstill, G. (1983) Resources and Responsibilities for Field Workers Amongst the Pitjantjatjara: Indulkana, South Austra-

lia, paper delivered to the Musicology Section of the 53rd ANZAAS
Congress, Perth
Maddock, K. (1974) *The Australian Aborigines: A portrait of their society*
London: Allen Lane
Moyle, R.M. (1979) *Songs of the Pintupi: Musical Life in a Central Australian
Society* Canberra: Australian Institute of Aboriginal Studies
—— (1986) *Alyawarra Music: Songs and Society in a Central Australian
Community* Canberra: Australian Institute of Aboriginal Studies
Munn, N. (1973) *Walbiri Iconography* Ithaca: Cornell University Press
Payne, H. (1984) 'Residency and Ritual Rights' in J.C. Kassler and J.
Stubington (eds) *Problems and Solutions: Occasional Essays in Musicology
presented to Alice M. Moyle* Sydney: Hale & Iremonger, pp. 264–78
Strehlow, T.G.H. (1971) *Songs of Central Australia* Sydney: Angus &
Robertson
White, I.M. (1974) 'Aboriginal women's status: A paradox resolved' in F.
Gale ed. *Women's Role in Aboriginal Society* 2nd edn, Canberra:
Australian Institute of Aboriginal Studies
—— (1977) 'From Camp to Village: Some Problems of Adaption' in R.M.
Berndt (ed.) *Aborigines and Change: Australia in the Seventies* Canberra:
Australian Institute of Aboriginal Studies
Wild, S.A. (1987) 'Recreating the Jukurrpa: Adaptation and Innovation of
Songs and Ceremonies in Warlpiri society' in M. Clunies-Ross, T.
Donaldson and S.A. Wild (eds) *Songs of Aboriginal Australia* Oceania
Monograph 32, Sydney: University of Sydney, pp. 97–120

# 3

# RITES FOR SITES OR SITES FOR RITES?

*The dynamics of women's cultural life in the Musgraves*

### Helen Payne

IN THIS paper I argue that one cannot appreciate women's relationship to, or knowledge of, sites without examining their relationship to, and knowledge of, rites and moreover, that in examining women's rites one must distinguish between ideal models articulated by women for their ritual practice and the actual realisation of such models in performances given by women.

I further contend that the relationship between ceremonies and land is not in the form of a simple 1 : 1 ratio such that 'those who own the songs own the land' (R. Moyle, 1983: 66) or such that 'ownership of "ceremonies" is a *sine qua non* for ownership of' land (R. Moyle, 1986: 4). Rather, women's rites are equatable to knowledge which one ' "holds" . . . "loses" . . . or passes on' (Myers, 1976: 400f) and as such, constitute resources of public importance to be won or lost through negotiation processes best termed 'politicking' (Swartz, 1968). These processes become particularly noticeable following the death of one publicly acknowledged as holding authoritative rights for rich, fertile country, that other women are desirous of securing for themselves (see Payne, 1988: 216ff).

The often protracted negotiation processes that serve to establish, maintain or lose women their rights to sites both thrive on, and themselves create, a 'lack of *strict* fit between the land rights of the rightful performers and the lands celebrated in the song series they rightfully perform' (Sutton, 1987: 82); that is, they ensure that a gap exists between ideal and actual in respect to women's ritual life.

## My participation in women's ritual life in the Musgraves

It was at Ernabella (for location see Map 3.1), situated on the eastern side of the Musgrave Ranges, that I received my first instruction in keeping/'holding' (Myers, 1976: 400ff) Aboriginal women's rites and sites. This initial instruction took place some 13 years ago. Since this time I have continued to receive instruction, either while living around the Musgraves or else while women from the Musgraves have been living with me, in Adelaide.

The majority of the women from whom I have received instruction identify themselves as Pitjantjatjara-speakers, but there are a few who classify themselves as Yankuntjatjara-speakers.[1]

My main instructors in women's life have been my 'close' sisters[2] whose rites and sites I have gradually become actively involved in 'keeping', not by my own choice but rather as a result of my role-casting by my teachers.[3] As Sutton and Rigsby (1982: 157) comment:

> a researcher . . . has a better chance of coming to grips with local politicks if he consciously recognizes that he is himself a political resource and if he develops an active involvement in them. This may not always be a matter of choice if one wishes to remain in the field.

A major part of my responsibility as a 'keeper' of women's rites is to ensure that information likely to stultify the growth or continuance of these rights is not made available to others without my teacher's permission. This paper has been returned to relevant women and both the Pukatja and Pitjantjatjara councils and that permission has been granted to me. However, as the placing of restrictions on dissemination of data constitutes a dynamic part of the culture practised by women in the Musgraves, I have chosen not to reveal the identity of women, sites or rites in this paper. I do not believe that in taking this precaution I will be eschewing data in

**Map 3.1   Location of place names in the text and, in shading, the geographic extent of Payne's participation in women's ritual life in the Musgraves**

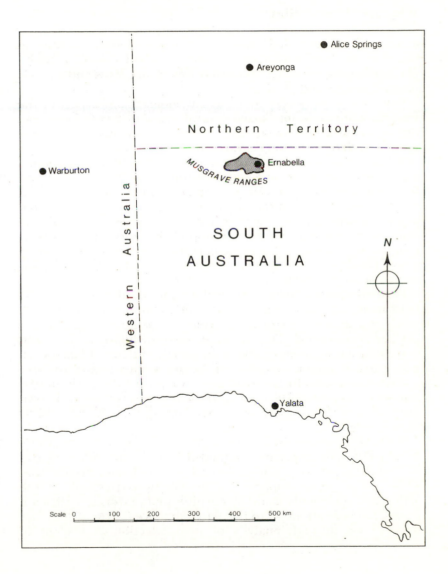

such a way as to misrepresent any analytical results. However, at the same time if any of my arguments appear 'to lack empirical support' I, like Hamilton (1979a: 238) must plead that this is unavoidable under the terms of my agreement—both ethical and legal—with Anangu Pitjantjatjaraku[4] (South Australia, 1981).

## What are women's rites?

In articulated form they constitute a series of texts or sites; in practice they comprise a simultaneous presentation of a multiplicity of phenomena, viz. musical forms, dance steps and actions, painted designs and objects.

For the enculturated person, at any moment one aspect of the rite may be brought into sharper aural, visual or tactile focus than the others and moreover, may serve to recall particular topographic and/or ancestral characteristics.[5]

A particular grouping or clustering of the above-mentioned aspects of a rite occurs in a ritual performance. The smallest unit for such a grouping I call an item. An item may comprise a simultaneous presentation of all, or some, of the above-listed aspects of a rite, and may be repeated several times in succession in order to permit dancers time to unfold the story (through their enactment). Usually a break in performance occurs to separate items. Breaks in performance may also occur during the performance of the one item.

Proceedings that include the performance of items interspersed with breaks in performance, and which continuously take place while at a selected performance venue, constitute what I term a performance session. This may last minutes, hours or days, and may feature enactment of one or hundreds of items. Thus several performance sessions may occur before women claim to have unfolded all events for a Dreaming because, for the enculturated listener or observer, each item unfolds only one event of the known life history of the ancestor or ancestral group thought responsible for creating it.

It has been asserted by Ellis et al. (1978: 72) and R. Moyle (1976: 5 and 1979: 9) that a pre-determined order of items is adhered to at all costs in a performance session. However, I have argued that while these authors appear to be taking cognisance of the articulated statements made by enculturated performers they are paying too little attention to the actual practice (Payne, 1988: 8). I have shown through analysis of item selection as evident in women's performance practice how the articulated item order for a Dreaming is *not* adhered to in the actual practice, even to the point of some articulated aspects of it *never* being realised in the latter (Payne, 1988: 204ff).


**What are women's sites?**

While to those enculturated in the traditions of Aboriginal culture, sites are those environmental features which bear constant testimony to the creative powers of the ancestors whose powers first shaped and now lie entrapped within them, analytically-speaking a site constitutes a topographic feature, often one of distinction. One might reasonably conclude that in desert Australia a distinctive environmental feature would be one constituting, or linked to, a water supply and hence possible vegetative abundance and animal life. On analysing the topograhic, geographic and economic significance of a series of sites said by enculturated performers to belong to the one Dreaming, I found that all Dreaming sites constituted a waterhole and/or a place of possible water retention and/or a vantage point from which to view surrounding countryside and/or a shelter (e.g. a cave), and that many of the sites offered more than one of the above advantages. Moreover, I found that these Dreaming sites were the only sites to have such characteristics within an otherwise arid desert terrain (Payne, 1988: 185ff).


**Sitemic relationships and their significance for women**

I have previously examined rite–site interconnection for a series of items claimed by enculturated performers to identify the one ancestral group (Payne, 1988: 170ff). The interconnection, which I termed 'sitemic', was such that an item named at least one site; but the converse did not apply. Rather, economically rich sites had one or more items associated with them, while comparatively infertile sites were often devoid of a sitemic relationship.

From observing the colours on a landsat satellite image aimed at showing, through variation in colour, the density–sparseness of vegetation, I found that as the sitemic relationship increased in the

Dreaming, so too did the fertility of the region. Moreover, I found that the Dreaming path followed the only major line of fertility in an otherwise arid environment (Payne 1988: 186).

From my observations of this landsat image I could readily see how a knowledge of a Dreaming could serve as a mnemonic aid for the recollection of economically fertile terrain in an otherwise arid region (Payne, 1984: 269). However, a Dreaming will only serve this function for those who have undergone the necessary training to equip them with such knowledge—knowledge vital to a hunting and gathering lifestyle and still necessary today for the maintenance of a tradition-oriented lifestyle.

### Processes of establishing, maintaining and retaining sitemic relationships

Women's ritual training ensures that women have visited sites for which their teachers claim knowledge and ownership rights, and that they know how to properly care for them, in both a physical and a spiritual sense.[6]

In the 1970s I noted that women had the least trouble recalling items that named economically rich sites (Payne, 1984: 271). I further found that such sites were indeed those most celebrated in women's performances (Payne, 1988: 205ff). Bell (1979: 22) records that it gives women power and status to be able to assert that their 'country is good country'. I have shown that because ritual activity intensifies at economically fertile sites, such that they are surrounded by items and thus theoretically can be sung into from all directions, women are aided in celebrating the bounty of their country by the structure of sitemic relationships (Payne, 1984: 269). However, it is the public reaction to item choices as presented in performance by an individual leader that determines *how* articulated sitemic relationships are realised in practice and thus how economic and spiritual fertility of sites is used to affirm/negate an individual's social status. This process constitutes 'politicking' for rights to 'sing into sites' (Bell, 1978: 5) and results in the type of negotiation processes outlined in Payne (1984: 272ff and 1988: 216ff).

I have evidence of new items being dreamt for the sites once held by a deceased woman, and found that the dreamers of these new items were either those women living closest to the sites they were seeking to claim or those that could emphasise, through various means,[7] both their connection with the sites and with the woman who had previously held the right to sing them (Payne, 1988:

216ff). At the same time as finding new Dreaming for the sites once held by the deceased woman, these same women were fighting counter claims for ownership of them. These counter claims were being advanced by women from a neighbouring community.

One of the ways in which the women residing at the site sought to ward off the challenges of the neighbouring group was to geographically 'realign' their new-found items such that they came to name more centrally-located and economically-important features present at the sites (rather than ones both further away from the centre of the sites and less economically significant). They did this through articulations of sitemic relationships (for these sites). In short, the dreamers 'moved' the geographic location of their new-found items such that they came to surround that part of the sites housing the most significant economic features (Payne, 1988: 216ff).

As the process is ongoing it is too early to foresee the outcome. However, the process already suggests that:

First in articulating sitemic relationships, items can remain constant while their geographic location is 'altered' by performers. (I have also found the reverse to be true, but the example of text substitution to which I later refer in this paper will exemplify this).

Second, there is no fixed immutable relationship between persons, rites and sites such as that suggested by R. Moyle (1983: 66). Rather, as Bell (1983a: 6) suggests, there is a need for interpretation of rites when they are presented as evidence of women's rights in land, and this should be carried out by those (ie dance ethnographers, ethnomusicologists etc) with the required 'specialized knowledge to read the "evidence" presented in this form.'

**Distinguishing between women's, men's and general business**

'The law is termed "business" and is made up of "women's business" and "men's business" ' (Bell, 1981: 319). There is also some business involving active participation by both males and females.

Hamilton (1979: 269), on noting as did White (1975) before her, the extreme separation of the sexes in desert life, comments that:

> this acute sexual separation has often been taken as an
> index of the degree to which women are second-rate citizens
> in Central Australian society. Considering the male secret
> life to be the pinnacle of social achievement, these observers

conclude that the rigid exclusion of women is a direct reflection of their social unimportance. The paradox is, however, that women in Central Australia have a flourishing secret life of their own. The existence of women's ceremonies has been noted by a number of observers, both male and female, but the general consensus is that these are matters of little general importance; their main focus is said to be love-magic and child-birth, which are seen as profoundly secular concerns without any 'spiritual' import whatever.

There are relatively few in-depth studies of women's ritual life and even less accurate documentation of their sites. This invisibility of women's ritual life in the literature is a reflection of male dominance—both in terms of the sex of the researcher and of the particular gender models endorsed by the researcher—in the collection of data. Bell (1982a: 10) suggests that although:

> [f] eminists have indicated areas of enquiry . . . the extreme
> separation of the sexes in desert society represents an analytic
> challenge which . . . is best met in the first instance by
> increasing our ethnographic understanding of women's
> domain.

Against this background it is very difficult, if not premature, to compare women's and men's business. Furthermore, just as 'no male white investigator has ever been able to get more than a faint hint of the women's mysteries in Central Australia' (Strehlow, 1971: 647), (although most do not acknowledge such in their writings (Bell, 1983b: 241)), so too, no female can ever hope to gain more than a faint hint of men's 'mysteries' in central Australia. This is not to suggest that members of the one sex do not *know* the secret material possessed by members of the other sex.[8]

Unlike R. Moyle (1979: 66f) who found the same songs in both women's and men's song series, but was not at liberty to tell the members of the opposite sex of this sharing between them, Strehlow (1971: 653) acknowledges the findings of his comparison of men's and women's healing charms. These revealed 'absolute identity in form, metre, and language' and led him to postulate that 'the language and the rhythms of the special women's songs must have come from the same sources which supplied the ingredients of the men's poetry.' Analytical validation of Strehlow's suggestion in other areas than rhythm and text may be an issue of interest to future historians (with access to well documented archival material); certainly it is not one affording easy examination at this time.

While I can only offer limited comment on distinctions between men's and women's items, it is openly acknowledged that men and women share common Dreaming sites, especially where these are of economic significance. Wild (1984: 199), in attempting to address the 'currently contentious' issue of gender relations through analysis of male–female performance roles cites *Yam Purlapa* as a suitable genre for investigating the issue, 'because it is the only genre in which men and women sing together'. His conclusion is that women take a less assertive role in this genre of ceremonial performance than do men.

However, because the Yam Purlapa that Wild uses to examine the issue of gender relations in performance is the acknowledged property of a male (Wild, 1984: 190), it follows that at least one male—this male or his nominee—will take charge of any performance of it. Conversely, it has been my experience that in women's ceremonies which have included participation by men, men could be said to be the less assertive participants (Payne, 1988: 45). In short, in the Musgraves, I have found no such phenomenon as a ceremony in which the sexes participate in equal measure. Moreover, as Bell suggests, it is premature to endorse a model of either sexual equality or male/female dominance, because we know so little of 'women's domain' (1983b: 241). 'We need to be clear regarding the nature of woman's contribution to her society, her rights and responsibilities, before we endorse one particular model of male-female as an accurate gloss on gender relations.' (Bell, 1982a: 10).

## Towards documentation of changes in women's cultural knowledge

While there has been an increasing number of 'spot' studies detailing Aboriginal women's contribution to society we are only just starting to cross-relate these to form a picture of Aboriginal woman's independent contribution to her society.

In my brief 13 years of study of Aboriginal women's life, I have seen enormous changes occur to the way in which women regard and practice their ritual life. What is not known is to what degree these changes have always been a feature of women's ritual life. It will only be through comparing the types of processes of change tabulated by me with those which have been, and continue to be, documented by others, that I (or others) can hope to answer this question.

I have compared tape recordings of items collected by other researchers and found in the latter many of the same items (musically and textually-speaking) as those sung to me by women of the Musgraves. A brief outline of the geographic locations, gender of singers and circumstances of performance for three such examples follows:

**Example 1**: Items X, Y, and Z, classified as secret, were performed by women in the Musgraves in both 1975 and 1978. I tape recorded both performances of them. I later found these same items present in tape recordings made by a female in the 1950s at Alice Springs. Here they were sung by men. They again appeared in tape recordings made by a male in the 1970s at Areyonga. Here they were sung by men, led by one of the same singers that had performed for the 1950s tape recording session.

**Example 2**: Items A, B and C, etc., classified as open, were performed by women in the Musgraves in both 1975 and 1978 and I tape recorded them at both times. I later found these same items, albeit in some cases with slightly altered textual syllables, in tape recordings made in the 1960s by a female at Warburton. Here they were classified as very secret. They also appeared in tape recordings made by females at various times during the 1960s at Yalata. From conversations with one of these females, it appears that the items were regarded as more secret at Yalata than they were in the Musgraves.

**Example 3**: I understand from conversations with one female researcher that she tape recorded, prior to 1975, items that I tape recorded in both 1975 and 1978 and that moreover, we worked with some of the same performers. She records that prior to 1975 these items were regarded as very secret. In 1975 and 1978 when I tape recorded them, they constituted open camp performances, directed by women but with men participating in the performances. From 1978 until the early 1980s they began to be classified as secret but women were not unilateral in their decision as to whether it was all items or just some which should be so classified by them.

In the early 1980s the acknowledged owner of these items died. As I had received considerable instruction in these items I became actively involved in the process of 'keeping' them. I learned this when the woman who wished to lay claim to the sites once held by the deceased informed me that she could not perform the items naming these sites without me and as I had not recently visited the Musgraves, this meant that she could only perform them in

Adelaide. This assertion ensured that these items received what amounted to a secret classification in the Musgraves.

The above examples show that items may be regarded as secret at one time or place but not at another, although the reasons why this may be so may be quite different for each example.

While Schebeck (1986: 52) suggests that one should not get involved in casting 'a value judgement about the justifiability of the political concept of secrecy in Aboriginal society' nonetheless, one needs to be aware that as the phenomenon exists, like the rest of culture, it will experience change. Moreover, this change may now occur either *within* the one residential and/or social group (example 3 above) or *between* residential and/or social groups (examples 1 and 2 above). It is possible that:

> women's items have a very wide currency and thus that learning items in a new residential region so as to validate one's claims to different sites [might be] more a question of politicizing for public approval of one's performance than of acquiring new performance techniques and structures. (Payne, 1988: 52)

Indeed, this contention had been pre-empted in Hamilton's suggestion (1979b: 14) that 'the relocation of people into another area could readily be brought about by attributing familiar-looking landscape features to known myth-cycles, and presumably by caching [sic] relevant sacred objects.' As on 'marriage women have always faced the possibility of living on country of which they have no direct experience' (Bell, 1982b: 29), Bell suggests that '[w]omen's ceremonies have always had the power to incorporate and transform.' The claim by Buckley et al. (1968: 25) that '[w]hen . . . neighbours infiltrated a territory, . . . they went even further in their infringement of the accepted rules, and validated their rights to totemic sites by claiming ownership of the associated rituals' implies that women's rites are different for each new-found territory and thus site-specific. Accordingly, this claim contrasts with those of Bell (1982b: 29); Hamilton (1979b: 14) and Payne (1988: 52) as cited above. However, my own findings are based on data collected some ten years later than that collected by Buckley et al. (1968) and at a time when women were beginning to assert their choices in residency to defy established virilocal residency patterns. Therefore, it may be that change has occurred in this aspect of women's lives. Nonetheless, Bell (1982b: 29) has argued that '[w]omen's ceremonies have *always* had the ability to incorporate and transform' (my own emphasis). It would seem, then, that the question remains whether this is not one of their distinguishing features?

Although I have already noted some changes in item classification in women's cultural life in the Musgraves, there have been many more, albeit of a different kind. For example:

1  I witnessed a complete text substitution: the singers having first sung the one text, then immediately, without hesitation, substituted another one, meanwhile maintaining all other aspects of the item structure, that is, dance forms, designs, etc. I noted that the substitution occurred in response to a grimace from one of the dancers. Much later I discovered (through checking several written records of genealogies kept by certain individuals in the area) that the name of this dancer's deceased brother constituted the same syllables as those sung in the initial singing of the item text. Moreover, the substituted item text did not contain these syllables. The question of where the substituted text came from so rapidly, and the complete ease of the substitution, raises issues crucially relevant to joint ethnomusicological and linguistic consideration, but the place for that is not in this paper.

2  In 1975 I was shown a women's Dreaming site comprising three standing trees. Two were mythical beings and the other an object that one of the mythical beings carried with her. In 1978 one of the beings had fallen over and was lying on the ground. The change in the site structure was bemoaned by those women who were showing it to me. Nonetheless, they expressed the hope that in time a new tree would grow to replace the fallen being. What happens if there is no new tree? Will the remaining two standing trees become the two mythical beings? Will women's ritual knowledge again incorporate change, this time that wrought by nature?

These last two examples serve as a further indication of the intricacies of change that I have observed in women's ritual knowledge over the past 13 years. It is apparent that meaningful documentation of change in women's cultural knowledge requires access to accurate recording of information over a period of time, while the interpretation of the changes requires a deep knowledge of processes employed by women.

## How to avoid the pitfalls of the past: future collection of women's cultural knowledge

While women or men can collect information on women's cultural knowledge, the level of their penetration of the subject will be different. Likewise, if one is not aware of the gender models one endorses one will document women's cultural knowledge to reflect that gender model without realising how it is influencing one's documentation process. It is often assumed that only women, and preferably those with two or more children, should collect information on female rites. Yet a woman with two children who views the world through the eyes of one acknowledging male supremacy is not likely to correct the bias we currently have in the literature, for example: '[a]s a woman, Munn certainly had access to the world of women but her focus [was] the ritual symbolism of men and her valued informants male, because in Nancy Munn's analysis men control[led] the keys to cosmic order' (Bell, 1982a: 9).

Only a woman will gain access to the deepest levels of meanings inherent in women's business. But she must be prepared to undergo the arduous ritual training which, for those born into the community, begins informally at babyhood.

It would be ideal if the woman was a mother of two or more children:

> However, lest it appear that one *must* have children in order to participate in women's business—a suggestion posited for example by Hamilton (1981: 79)—and that therefore barren women *must* be excluded from it, I hasten to add that having children is by no means the *only* means by which senior Aboriginal women judge readiness to receive knowledge about, and assume responsibility in, their business. When a woman has participated in training for some time she is expected to gain in wisdom and to have learnt what she has been taught and begun to apply it. When she fails to apply what she has learnt, she is reprimanded, 'called mad or deaf' (Bell, 1983c: 35)[9] and her training stagnates until such time as she can show readiness to produce the right behavioural responses. This judgement applies equally to those who have borne children as to those who have not. Nonetheless, by and large, the path of having children and thus proving one's fertility in the non-ritual work sphere may be seen to complement one's gaining of ritual knowledge and subsequent proving of one's fertility—as a dreamer—in the ritual work sphere. Both types of fertility are considered equally vital to the survival and maintenance of the well-being of life in tradition-orientated society. (Payne, 1988: 78f)

Training continues for a woman until menopausal years when, if her progress has been satisfactory, she can expect to become involved in the process of establishing her own fertility as a dreamer.

Throughout training women's performance roles are graded until finally one takes command of the painting, dancing and singing processes, that is, the calling and negation of Dreaming powers. Restricted categories of ritual knowledge are given to those judged by older women as being ready to receive them. These categories comprise curative and *illpintji* knowledge. This latter I have argued operates as a mechanism through which social and emotional balance is maintained in a community and in order to do this, draws on the land-based affiliations of individuals (Payne, 1988: 87ff). (Too often women's rituals have been viewed as 'just' comprising love-making/*illpintji/yilpintji* etc. rituals which although greatly feared by men, are portrayed as not seriously affecting community operations).

The female undertaking the documentation who endorses the concept of going through the ritual training summarised above must have access to a vehicle if she is to take women to their sites.[10]

At women's sites she must be prepared to listen to mythology, watch ritual enactments, record analytical site details and attend to numerous other requests. As women find it difficult to maintain contact with their country often because of lack of independent access to vehicles some may be visiting the site for the first time, while others may be renewing their contact with it after a lengthy period of absence. Thus, it is often inappropriate on an initial visit to a site to take measurements, photographs, etc. such as are necessary for the accurate recording for the site position.[11]

If the first few visits to any sites of Dreaming significance for women may be taken up with appreciating the mythical significance of the site and person-place attachments, then it is absolutely *essential* that the female undertaking the documentation budgets for more than one visit to each site and then, recognising that as most items have sites, acknowledges that there will be a limit to the number of items and hence Dreaming sites she can accurately document in a given time.

It has been my experience that when a person shifts from community to community he or she is thought to be shifting allegiances and accordingly no community entrusts him or her with their secrets. As a result he or she fails to uncover the intricacies of the politicking processes that operate to transmit knowledge in any one of these communities.

I thus suggest that participation in day to day community life is best located in the one community. Documentation in one community has the potential to display depth, and if in-depth studies are carried out in several communities by different individuals, then there will be established a basis from which to conduct a comparative study of contemporary women's cultural knowledge. If the findings of a comparative study of contemporary women's cultural knowledge are then compared with the findings made by those collected at earlier dates we will have the opportunity to increase 'our ethnographic understanding of women's domain' which, after all, Bell (1982a: 10) suggests should be the first step we take in meeting the 'analytic challenge' presented by 'the extreme separation of the sexes in desert society.'

If the woman undertaking the documentation has not been born into the community in which she is operating, then she will need to determine the extent—geographic, social, economic, cultural, etc.—of that community. She also will need to be prepared to carry out her part in the obligations implied in the kinship structures into which she inevitably will be incorporated when accepted by the members of that community.[12]

It has been my experience that Aboriginal women are very patient, sustaining teachers, as I am sure it will be the experience of any sensitive woman who shows readiness to learn from them what it is like to be one of them. Those who go knowing nothing, with little knowledge of what they are about to receive, can be assured that the training they receive will be rigorous but rewarding and that the sisters, aunts, nieces, grandmothers, mothers and grand-daughters they acquire will serve to continue that education for them.

**Notes**

1  As 'there is a *de facto* relationship between a particular territory and a particular dialect' (Hamilton, 1982: 98), this distinction may be of significance when considering women's land-based relationships.
2  At Ernabella I was incorporated into the kinship system and given sisters, brothers and other family members. Some of these were 'close' family members, others were more 'distant' ones.
3  Compare accounts by Koning (1980); McAllester (1984) and Reay (1970).
4  The name accorded those having an interest in that area of land granted with freehold title in 1981 by the South Australian government.

5   The particular expression used to articulate this mnemonic associ-
    ation will depend on the linguistic affiliation of the speaker (C. Ellis,
    1969: 7 and C. Ellis et al., 1978: 69).
6   'The maintenance of a site requires both physical caring—for
    example the rubbing of rocks or clearing of debris—and the
    performance of items aimed at caring for the spirit housed at it.
    Without these maintenance processes the site remains, but is said to
    lose the spirit held within it. It is then said to die and all those who
    share physical features and spiritual connections with it are then also
    thought to die. Thus, to ensure the well-being of life, sites must be
    cared for and rites performed to keep alive the dreaming powers
    entrapped within them. The responsibility to carry out this work falls
    on the shoulders of those who, firstly, have undergone the training
    necessary to enable them to execute their duties effectively, and
    secondly, have received, and continue to receive, public ratification
    for their execution of these duties.' (Payne, 1988: 72).
7   Bell (1983b: 51) states that '[w]omen trace their relationship to the
    ancestral heroes and thus to the land, in a number of ways. Through
    mother, father, place of birth, conception and residence flow
    qualitatively different rights and responsibilities.
8   See, for example, accounts by Kaberry (1939: 228f); Strehlow (1971:
    653); White (1975: 125f) and Payne (1988: 49).
9   Bell (1983c) is Bell (1983b) in this paper.
10  See Bell (1978: 15) and Payne (1984: 273).
11  I argue that in Aboriginal culture one needs to record the three
    dimensions of sites. In order to achieve this type of recording I use
    pairs of aerial photographs. These I view stereoscopically so that I can
    obtain an accurate set of co-ordinates for the positioning of each site.
    When these site position markings are later transferred onto large-
    scale maps, the overall result using this method affords greater
    accuracy in site recording than does the recording of site positions
    directly onto the small-scale (1:250 000) maps.
12  For accounts of incorporation see Payne (1988: 56ff), Reay (1970)
    and White et al. (1985).

**References**

Bell, D. (1978) The Alyawarra and Kaititja Land Claim [of the Central
    Land Council]: A Statement, 6th October, 1978 and A Second
    Statement, 16th October, 1978, Canberra: Australian Institute of
    Aboriginal Studies Library
—— (1979) The Pawurrinji Puzzle: A Report to Central Land Council on
    the Country of Pawurrinji, Canberra: Australian Institute of Abori-
    ginal Studies Library
—— (1981) 'Women's Business is Hard Work: Central Australian Abori-
    ginal Women's Love Rituals' *Signs: Journal of Women in Culture and
    Society* 7, pp. 314–337

—— (1982a) Aboriginal Women and the Religious Experience, The Young Australian Scholar Lecture Series Charles Strong Memorial Trust, Adelaide: Australian Association for the Study of Religions

—— (1982b) 'In the Tracks of the Munga Munga' Canberra: Australian Institute of Aboriginal Studies Library

—— (1983a) Aboriginal Women and Land: Learning from the Northern Territory Experience, paper read at Workshop on Aboriginal Land Rights, University of Western Australia, Canberra: Australian Institute of Aboriginal Studies Library

—— (1983b) *Daughters of Dreaming* Melbourne: McPhee Gribble/George Allen & Unwin

Buckley, R., Ellis, C.J., Hercus, L.A. and White, I.M. (1968) 'Group Project on Andagarinja Women' Vol. 2 Adelaide: private publication, University of Adelaide Library

Ellis, C.J. (1969) 'Structure and Significance in Aboriginal Song' *Mankind* 7, pp. 3–14

—— (1985) *Aboriginal Music: Education for Living: Cross-Cultural Experiences from South Australia* St. Lucia: University of Queensland Press

Ellis, C.J. and Brunton, J (In Press) 'From the Dreaming Rock to Reggae Rock' in A.D. McCredie (ed.) *From Colonel Light into the Footlights: the performing arts in South Australia from 1836 to the present* Adelaide: Pagel Press

Ellis, C.J., Ellis, A.M., Tur, M. and McCardell, A (1978) 'Classification of sounds in Pitjantjatjara-speaking areas' *Australian Aboriginal Concepts* ed. L.R. Hiatt. Canberra: Australian Institute of Aboriginal Studies pp. 68–80

Hamilton, A. (1979a) Timeless Transformation: Women, Men and History in the Australian Western Desert, Phd Thesis, University of Sydney

—— (1979b) Women and Land (typescript) Resource Centre, Australian Institute of Aboriginal Studies

—— (1981) 'A Complex Strategical Situation: Gender and Power in Aboriginal Australia' in N. Grieve and P. Grimshaw (eds) *Australian Women: Feminist Perspectives* Melbourne: Oxford University Press, pp. 69–85

—— (1982) 'Desecended from Father, Belonging to Country: Rights to Land in the Australian Western Desert' in E.B. Leacock and R.B. Lee (eds) *Politics and history in band societies* Cambridge: Cambridge University Press pp. 85–108

Kaberry, P.M. (1939) *Aboriginal Woman: Sacred and Profane* London: Routledge

Koning, J. (1980) 'The Fieldworker as Performer: Fieldwork Objectives and Social Roles in County Clare, Ireland' *Ethnomusicology* 24, pp. 417–429

McAllester, D.P. (1984) 'A Problem in Ethics' in J.C. Kassler and J. Stubington (eds) *Problems and Solutions: Occasional Essays in Musicology presented to Alice M. Moyle* Sydney: Hale and Iremonger pp. 279–289

McCardell, A. (1976) Rhythm and Melody in Australian Aboriginal Songs of the Western Desert, PhD Thesis, University of Western Australia

Moyle, R.M. (1976) 'Pintupi Music: Songs from Australia's Central Desert' Canberra: Australian Broadcasting Commission.

——— (1979) *Songs of the Pintupi: Musical Life in a Central Australian Society* Canberra: Australian Institute of Aboriginal Studies.

——— (1983) 'Songs, Ceremonies and Sites: The Agharringa Case' N. Peterson and M. Langton (eds) *Aborigines, Land and Land Rights* Canberra: Australian Institute of Aboriginal Studies, pp. 66–93

Moyle, R.M. with the help of Slippery Morton, Alyawarra interpreter (1986) *Alyawarra Music: Songs and Society in a central Australian Community* Canberra: Australian Institute of Aboriginal Studies

Myers, F.R. (1976) 'To Have and To Hold': A Study of Persistence and Change in Pintupi Social Life, Phd Thesis, Bryn Mawr College, Bryn Mawr

Payne, H. (1978) 'The Integration of Music and Belief in Australian Aboriginal Culture' *Religious Traditions: A New Journal in the study of Religion* 1, pp. 8–18

——— (1980) 'Transmission of Extra-Musical Information in Traditional Pitjantjatjara Music: The Significance for Processing of Acoustical Data of Australian Aboriginal Music' *Tenth International Congress on Acoustics, Vol. 7: Invited Papers, Structured Session papers* Sydney: Australian Acoustical Society, pp. 146–149

——— (1984) 'Residency and Ritual Rights' in J.C. Kassler and J. Stubington (eds) *Problems and Solutions: Occasional Essays in Musicology presented to Alice M. Moyle* Hale and Iremonger, pp. 264–278

——— (1988) Singing a Sister's Sites: Women's Rites in the Australian Musgrave Ranges, Phd Thesis, University of Queensland

Pritam, P. (Antony McCardell) (1980) 'Aspects of Musical Structure in Australian Aboriginal Songs of the South-West of the Western Desert' *Studies in Music* 14, pp. 9–44

Reay, M. (1970) 'A Decision as Narrative' in R.M. Berndt (ed) *Australian Aboriginal Anthropology: Modern Studies in the Social Anthropology of the Australian Aborigines* Nedlands: University of Western Australia Press, Australian Institute of Aboriginal Studies, pp. 164–173

Schebeck, B. (1986) 'After successful field work: what to do with all the "material"?' *Australian Aboriginal studies* 1, pp. 52–58

South Australian Government (1981) *Pitjantjatjara Land Rights Act* Adelaide: Government Printer

Strehlow, T.G.H. (1971) *Songs of Central Australia* Sydney: Angus and Robertson

Sutton, P. and Rigsby, B. (1982) 'People with "Politicks": Management of Land and Personnel on Australia's Cape York Peninsula' in N.M. Williams and E.S. Hunn (eds) *Resource Managers: North American and Australian Hunter-Gatherers* AAAS Selected Symposium 67 Colorado: Westview Press, pp. 155–171

Sutton, P. (1987) 'Mystery and Change' in M. Clunies-Ross, T. Donaldson, S.A. Wild (eds) *Songs of Aboriginal Australia* Oceania Monograph 32, Sydney: University of Sydney, pp 97–120

Swartz, M.J. ed. (1968) *Local-Level Politics: Social and Cultural Perspectives* Chicago: Aldine
White, I.M. (1975) 'Sexual Conquest and Submission in the Myths of Central Australia' in L.R. Hiatt (ed.) *Australian Aboriginal Mythology* Canberra: Australian Institute of Aboriginal Studies, pp. 123–142
White, I., Barwick D. and Meehan, B (eds) (1985) *Fighters and Singers: the lives of some Australian Aboriginal women* Sydney: Allen and Unwin
Wild, S.A. (1984) 'Warlbiri Music and Culture: Meaning in a Central Australian Song Series' in J.C. Kassler and J. Stubbington (eds) *Problems and Solutions: Occasional Essays in Musicology presented to Alice M. Moyle* Sydney: Hale and Iremonger, pp. 186–203

# 4

# DIGGING DEEP

*Aboriginal women in the Oodnadatta region of South Australia in the 1980s*

### Jen Gibson

THE TOWNSHIP of Oodnadatta celebrates its centenary in 1990. The wider region has been settled by Europeans for even longer. What remains of Aboriginal life has undergone radical change. Similar patterns of colonisation and post-colonial society are found throughout Australia. Yet individual differences remain, and in another equally true sense each region is unique. I welcome this opportunity to share my experiences of the life and personality of Aboriginal women in Oodnadatta today.

On our first visit to Oodnadatta in 1985 Bruce Shaw (my husband) and I were driven out to Hamilton Station, 100 kilometres north of the town, where three of the most senior community members live in pleasant bush surroundings beside two newly constructed log cabins. As evening fell they broke into song, remembering what it was like on nearby Macumba Station and elsewhere in the days when 20 or more men sat around in a large group with boomerangs clapping and the women painted in white ochre danced naked in the firelight. The singing that evening was vibrant with life, vitality and joy. In some ways it sounded harsh, like the call of a crow in the bush—powerful and dynamic. All this was sustained by three very elderly people, a fusion of past and present within this natural environment, arising as from the earth itself.

Speaking of the Western Desert peoples, Strehlow (1965: 132) too found: 'The most striking thing about these people was their ready laughter—they were a cheerful, laughing people, who bore themselves as though they had never known a care in the world'. It is glimpses such as these, of older women and men today, that hint at a fragile continuity of culture.

This continuity is of vital importance, not only for the few old folk themselves, but for younger relatives and members of the Aboriginal community at Oodnadatta and elsewhere. While three old people with a continual stream of visiting relatives and friends continue to live at Hamilton Station, there is a meaningful and vital link sustained for all. This is maintained by older people of both genders and involves mutual support and respect, together with a little teasing.

There is a recognition of the privacy of men's and women's business. When four women went collecting firewood there was spontaneous dancing and singing of part of a women's dance including cupping hands to beat a rhythm, crouching down and joking about sexual matters. Clearly such a situation was best enjoyed amongst members of the same gender. Trips on which only women were present were happy and intimate occasions with considerable chatter and joking. The midday dinner camp was the focus of real enjoyment both for the good feed and the companionship. When men were present women appeared equally pleased and joking and laughter were shared.

The area around Oodnadatta was originally Arabana, Southern Arrernte and Wangkangurru territory, marking the northern boundary for the Arabana and the southern boundary of the southern Arrernte and the western boundary of the Wangkangurru. Antikirinja, Matutjara, and Yankuntjatjara, also referred to as Alurijta or Loritja, peoples have links with the other Western Desert peoples, especially the Pitjantjatjara. They came more recently to the Oodnadatta region from the west and north after 1904. In the 1940s R. and C. Berndt observed the town situation at Oodnadatta in detail as part of their study of Aborigines' changing circumstances. A semi-sacred ceremony which was held at 'race weekend' contained Arrernte and Antikirinja elements. Nearly all the men, women and children participated, with older women playing a significant role (1951: 147–190). Regrettably these ceremonies no longer occur spontaneously around Oodnadatta itself, though they do occasionally take place out at Hamilton Station.

Buckley, Ellis, Hercus, Penny and White in 1967 compiled a two-volume report entitled 'A Group Project on Andagarinja Women'. Women's secret ritual and ceremonial role, independent yet complementary to that of men, is clearly documented by this study. The song and dance cycles pass from Alice Springs, through to Oodnadatta and thence Coober Pedy, along kinship networks. These gatherings were important in traditional terms for the secular purpose of coming together and keeping regular contact with one another and for the sacred reasons of maintaining law, love magic and Dreaming.

The following 20 years have shown quite pronounced changes in women's traditional knowledge. Of approximately 30 women listed as being involved in various ceremonies in the mid-1960s only five were known by me to be in the Oodnadatta area at the time of my own visits there from 1985 to 1987. One was by then over 85 years old. Two women had been children in the 1960s, another was now blind and a fifth drank heavily and hence she forgot much traditional knowledge. The impact of Western Desert languages is evidenced in the women's regular use of words of this origin (which I have followed here), even though they or their parents originally spoke Arrente, Wangkangurru or Arabana.

At the present time there is a very low proportion of women and men between the ages of 40 and 65 years. Many people of this age group have died from alcohol-related cause—illnesses and accidents. Others have left the area, many moving to larger centres such as Coober Pedy, Port Augusta and Alice Springs, or to smaller ones like Finke, Birdsville, Indulkana and Ernabella, where they have strong family ties. In 1986 Oodnadatta township had a population of 159, comprised of 87 males and 72 females. In 1981 there were 163 in the town, of whom 87 were male and 76 female. Approximately 60 per cent of these residents were listed as Aboriginal in the census figures. Even more have Aboriginal links by descent or marriage. It is interesting to observe the age of people of Aboriginal descent in the 1986 census. Thirteen were between birth and four years; sixteen between 5 and 14 years; thirteen between 15 and 19 years; thirty-two between 20 and 39; sixteen between 40 and 59, while only three were over sixty.

Macumba Station, 40 kilometres north-west of Oodnadatta, is the area best known to most women over the greatest length of time. It has been an important meeting place for members of the tribal and language groups mentioned above, not only traditionally but also in terms of pastoral employment. It is the country most women have the strongest associations with in the Oodnadatta area. Today, however, even this is fast becoming a thing of the past. Now no Aboriginal families live there, though a few Aboriginal stockmen work there. Of ten women with whom I associated most closely, six have strong links to Macumba. One, now very aged, came from further north around the Finke river and a second works on stations with her stockman husband, usually north of Hamilton. A third was born at Anna Creek Station to the south, while the fourth has early links with the town.

Ernest Kempe, an early owner/manager of Macumba, was associated with the station for many years from about 1900 to the 1930s.

> The blacks informed me he wrote that the creek now known as the Macumba, was once thickly timbered. A fire broke out at the head of it and took some days to reach the locality of Macumba Station. . . It is significant that every old tree along the Macumba Creek has been charred by fire. The waterhole upon which my head station is situated is called *Abma-arakata*, meaning 'snake mouth'. (Cockburn 1984: 133f)

On a visit to Macumba Station in 1985 this was confirmed by three of the women of southern Arrernte/Wangkangurru descent. Past the station homestead is *uralatuka*, the Fire Dreaming creek. One woman's son was born in this vicinity and hence is named *Tjornaka* because of his association with this dreaming. Luise Hercus (personal communication), say *suralatuka* means 'fire-stick' and refers specifically to Ooranalatica waterhole and by extension may be used to refer to the whole creek.

A large old box gum tree on the left, almost at the present Macumba homestead, beside the creek, was recognised as being associated with the Snake Dreaming. 'You see that great tree, *angkara*. . . . Before we born that tree been. . . That one is Snake Dreaming, dry one, old one now.' The small, younger *angkara* beside the old dry tree is also confirmed as a Snake Dreaming place.

A daughter of one of these women last visited this site in 1968. She recalled: 'There's an old gum tree in Macumba Station alone at the waterhole. That's where there were snakes'. Her statement indicates that some knowledge and interest continues amongst the under 40s age group. However, the extent and accuracy of such knowledge decreases over time as snippets of information are communicated out of context.

Visiting a Snake Dreaming site, the little snakes in the form of small rocks could be seen standing upright. These must on no account be touched as it would result in a great increase of snakes everywhere. This site belonged to a deceased brother of one woman. The site was in some disrepair as many of the snakes had fallen over.

There can be a physical connection between the site and the people associated with it. One of the younger folk in Oodnadatta explained:

> That's my Mum's Dreamtime story and my uncle's. . . And the people like . . . we all have in our body a birth mark [of] a snake's head. That's our Dreaming. I have my Dreamtime Snake head on my leg [on the right thigh]. They all have this little white patch—all [male and female family members born at Macumba] have this Dreamtime birth mark on us.

The older women were happy to have an opportunity to revisit Macumba. A significant part of this involved recalling memories and associations.

> Here is old bore. Nothing now. When I was a little kid lying around the bore, swimming. They had plenty of water, bore was running. Trough was there. . . It was nice bore, lovely. After then, when the bore was still here Audrey, June, Freddie, Arthur, Christopher [her own children], they used to play there.

One of these children, now in her late 30s, recalled her own memories of Macumba:

> My mother was born in Macumba. One gum tree—I've forgotten what name they call it in Arrernte. Well this is a new generation and people are forgetting all those things. . . . There's a [Dreamtime story] about a dingo. Mum only used to tell me about that. She used to sing it to us and tell us about this dingo story.

This woman's mother was mentioned by Buckley et al in the 1960s as not participating in the ceremonies they observed (even though she was present). Some 20 years later her children and others of the same age group have a considerably reduced repertoire of traditional stories and ceremonial knowledge.

In the vicinity of Oodnadatta there are many traditional sites known to the women. *Walurka* sandhills contain a Dreaming spot where I was told one woman went for the birth of her children. Old camp sites can be found there too. *Angkara nyinda* (one gum tree) soakage is closer to the town and was used by Aboriginal people in earlier times as their source of water. There are several different and now disused soakages in this creek. The original one is still marked by a now-dead tree. Another woman gave birth to a son on the outskirts of the town near a Frog Dreaming site.

The broad area around Dalhousie hot springs is the traditional country for some of the Oodnadatta women and their descendants. There used to be a large Aboriginal camp at Mt Dare, 'Tin Shanty' as it was known by the older people. Southern Arrernte crossed the boarder from Charlotte Waters and the Finke in the Northern Territory and Wangkangurru people came from Lake Eyre basin and the Western Desert.

At Dalhousie part of the Perentie (giant monitor lizard, the largest of the *varanus* species) Dreamtime history was recounted in connection with our revisiting the sites. We visited the place where Perentie had separated the dark and fair-skinned women, making off with the lighter coloured ones. There was the same interest and satisfaction as a Hindu would derive from reliving events from the Mahabarata. A Mosquito Dreaming, apparently associated with Abminga further north was discussed. We camped the night near the hot pool, *Idnyundra* of the Kingfisher Dreamtime history. Legends of the stars were recalled as we sat by the embers of our evening campfire.

The women belonging to this country revisited it with pride. 'I got a lotta water, more than [those other women]. And that nother Dalhousie, old house, that's mine again. My father was workin [on the] station when he was young feller, first he bin come from Birdsville.' There were sad memories too. The group of trees near the three *Angkada* (sleepy lizard) hills was where the women's father's camel had returned after many days, without its rider, thereby notifying his wife and family of his murder. It was there too after his death that one daughter was born within sight of the grey, red and black *Angkada* hills.

Elsewhere in the Dalhousie region was another pool, also with bubbles, where many old Aranda people used to swim. Their camps were nearby. In the sandhills is a charcoal site used by a grandfather of some of the women. Old Aboriginal bone fragments, probably ribs, bleached white but clearly from two human bodies, were identified by the women here.

In the revisiting and retelling of the history associated with each area and group of sites the women maintain and sustain the continuity of attachment. Even when women accompanying us visit a location for the first time they are renewing family links to the particular area. As people pass away others acquire rights and responsibilities in locations not originally theirs. This means there is at least someone to care for it and pass on some knowledge to younger generations.

For instance, an Aboriginal man originally from the central Northern Territory acquired special knowledge of an area north of Oodnadatta through long and intimate association with its senior custodians. Because of his interest the information was passed to him, together with the obligation to care for that region. Women with closer links by birth than he recognise his greater knowledge and make use of it. This has also occurred between Oodnadatta and Marree when Antikirinja people assume important roles in Arabana areas.

## European influences

Outside influences have impinged markedly on the Oodnadatta region since the mid-19th century. These commenced with the exploration of John McDouall Stuart in 1859. The route he mapped was adopted for the Overland Telegraph Line, which was completed in 1872. Many hundreds of square miles were also taken up as pastoral leases from this time on.

The decision to locate a town in the Neales River country followed plans to extend the northern railway from Warrina. On October 30, 1890, Oodnadatta was proclaimed a Government Township and in 1891 the railway was opened for traffic. The town immediately took on major importance as the railhead for the north. Chinese people moved into the area and established successful market gardens south of the town around Hookeys Hole.

Camels were introduced and with them came people from north India, Pakistan and Afghanistan, known locally as 'Afghans'. In the course of time the train also became known as the 'Ghan'. By 1895 there were 400 camels. Pack camels carried heavy loads better than horses over the dry terrain. Camels carried the Royal Mail to Alice Springs until the railway was extended there from Oodnadatta in 1929. Teams of camels travelled 900 miles north to Newcastle Waters and sometimes further. They also went west and east.

These developments were a disruption to Aboriginal traditional life over the whole of the north of South Australia and into the Northern Territory, but particularly around Oodnadatta itself. Doris Blackwell (nee Bradshaw) accompanied her parents as a young girl, through Oodnadatta en route to Alice Springs in 1899.

> Desolation was every where . . . A handful of galvanized iron buildings represented the State's most northerly town . . .
> Chained to the post by their wrists were six or seven natives . . . We were told that they had been caught spearing cattle . . .

chained together by their wrists, and at night by their ankles · as well, [they] had walked every step of more than three hundred miles to the railhead [from Alice Springs]. (1965: 25–26)

As well as white justice (these prisoners were en route to gaol at Port Augusta), diseases such as measles, influenza, whooping cough and venereal disease decimated the local groups. Elkin in 1931 (pp. 51–52) estimated less than 400 individuals remained of 19 tribes. 'The population of the whole region [north from Port Augusta] eighty years ago could hardly have been less than 3,000.' Yet there is no significant oral history of major killings or massacres around Oodnadatta or Marree.

Many Aboriginal people today trace their descent to Chinese, Irish, English or Afghan forbears. Fred Ah Chee (typescript Ah Chee & Shaw 1985) recalls:

They associated or solicited with Aboriginal women . . . It was the Aboriginal women who did all the washing, all the house work, and this is where the part-coloured originated. So they actually played a part in the destruction of Aboriginal people even though they were pioneers . . . Oh it's so complicated.

In turn the telegraph line, station life, the railway, the town itself with its facilities and government rations, the Australian Inland Mission hostel/hospital, European education, the influence of missionaries and the removal of part-Aboriginal children, produced enormous changes in the lives of Aboriginal people of both genders. Today Aboriginal children have to move away for high school and tertiary education, usually to Port Augusta or Adelaide.

Almost all people today speak Antikirinja. Some of the women also retain a little knowledge of Arrernte and Wangkangurru and Arabana, but this is slight and must be recalled for a specific site or plant. All children speak English from the time they attend pre-school at three or four years old. Many converse with their families in Antikirinja at home, making them, to an extent, bilingual. This is in contrast to Marree to the south, where Arabana is rarely used now except occasionally by a small handful of older people.

**Examining the details**

I have described some of the surviving knowledge of women living in and around Oodnadatta and the links with specific localities which are renewed whenever an opportunity is available. I will now turn to Aboriginal patterns of behaviour which may not be as obvious. Small details of daily life reveal so much, showing some continuity with traditions and practices of the past. 'It is only when one has noted the intensely human commonplaces of any people's existence' says Ruth Benedict, an early American cultural anthropologist, 'that one appreciates at its full importance the anthropologist's premise that human behaviour . . . is *learned* in daily living . . . If the search took me into trivial details of daily intercourse, so much the better. That was where people learned. (1967: 8)

When collecting genealogies, one of the details that I noticed was that in one family the four sons were all married to, or had been married to, four daughters from another family. The recurring European surname first attracted my attention to a pattern of sibling marriage exchange which is most certainly not European in origin. This pattern was also evident in other family trees. (Gibson 1987: Macumba Genealogy 11, Russell Genealogy 21, Stewart Genealogy 17.)

The Arabana, Wangkangurru and Diyari trace descent through the mother, having two (matrilineal) moiety divisions. One's marriage partner comes from the opposite group or moiety to oneself and one's mother (Elkin 1940: 372). Further, from Howitt's earlier observations we know that the practice of sister exchange is a traditional one (1904: 177) which remains amongst the Oodnadatta folk today, even though the traditional marriage rules are broken through cultural contact and movement of tribal groups.

I also observed on meeting folk at Oodnadatta in 1985 that a number of men and women had their two top front teeth missing. While this occurrence is by no means universal, it is sufficiently prevalent to be noticeable. Most of the women with teeth missing are in the older age group, by Oodnadatta standards, that is to say over 40. Tooth evulsion is the removal of the two upper front teeth and was the beginning of the initiatory path for girls and boys between the ages of eight and twelve years for the Diyari and Southern Arrernte (Howitt 1891: 79–84).

**Skill with plants and animals**

Some knowledge of bush plants is retained. Women identify and collect samples of trees, bushes and plants. Sometimes their memory proved faulty. Names were given in Antikirinja and/or in Arrernte along with a common English name which was usually known. Often instructions were fairly specific as to which part of the plant could be used to make medicines. *Arata*, known commonly in English as tar bush and botanically as *Eremophila freelingii* is like kerosene.

When you light him this one, kerosene fire. This one half
medicine. When you got manage you got to have a bath with
this one. Boil em, boil em, boil em. Still we use this one.
Sore all over, that's [the] medicine again . . . we can make a
firewood, this tree now *arata*.

The boiled liquid is also drunk to treat colds.

The grandchildren of the women have some knowledge of bush
food. Three girls under twelve were locating and digging up *yalka*,
native onions, unsupervised near the Oodnadatta dam late in 1987.
They said it tasted better roasted but since there was no fire they
were happy eating *yalka* raw. The taste was sweetish and fibrous
but quite pleasant.

Skill in catching traditional food is retained to some extent by a
few of the senior women. Children accompanying the women to
the sandhills are shown the tracks of a snake, an emu, a perentie, a
smaller lizard *angkada*, and whatever else is visible. Reader (1983:
48) illustrates with a photograph how an adult informs a child. A
child is seen examining a baby kangaroo with the caption 'Irene's
education begins "Here, look here, *Malu Tjapu*" no further
instruction is given'.

As the child observes the plant, animal or other environmental
or social feature within its natural context the adult simply supplies
its name without unnecessary conversation. A similar approach
successfully developed by Dr Maria Montessori an Italian educator
has spread to schools world-wide today (Montessori 1948: 145). If
early childhood experiences such as this were more regular,
traditional skills of bushcraft would survive more extensively.

Now women use an iron rod to tap on the surface of the ground
for a hollow sound indicating that burrows lie beneath. When a
rabbit was located in a general area, a long stick was found and one
end roughly broken before it was inserted. If the rabbit was
trapped a few hairs from its fur would be seen on the jagged end of
the stick. Having located it exactly dogs and women with their iron
bars then dig it out. When big game such as kangaroo, emu or perentie are caught today, it is usually with a rifle. One woman
requested that I purchase one for her.

Individuals are recognised as specially good damper makers or
cooks of fish. Traditional and western cuisine combine, as on one
occasion when the fish was stuffed with tomato, capsicum and
lemon salt and covered in tinfoil. It was then buried carefully in the
hot ashes and turned lovingly and finally removed and placed on a
bed of fresh gum leaves and dusted to remove the sand and ash.

People used to grind flour from local grasses to prepare damper
or johnnycakes. Wheat flour purchased from the store is used

universally now. Witchedy grubs were found in shrubs and trees by inserting a piece of wire with a hook on the end into holes in the branches or trunk and also by digging under roots, sometimes to the destruction of a shrub.

Traditionally animals were singed over the big fire and then cooked in the embers, covered with a lot of earth and ashes and turned part way through the cooking process. Younger folk in the town still consider this the 'correct' way of preparing and eating such animals. It is considered incorrect to cook them in an oven as it can bring misfortune to the community in the form of illness, accident or even death. Should one of these events occur someone will attribute it to this custom having been violated.

> You know this all the people here, Oodnadatta not allowed to skin a kangaroo. That's in the black fellow rule because the kangaroo is *anungu* [Aboriginal person] himself. This is [Wangkangurru] and [Arrernte] way. You got to cook him in the ashes. And Antikirinja rule again. That's Dreaming kangaroo! Only white fellow can skin em. No aborigine. That one [law] bin in all the time. [Two local men] skinning that kangaroo that's why all them wild *kurdaicha* men bin coming here [from across the Northern Territory border. You are] not allowed to skin em. You can't tell [those boys] nothing. They won't believe you. They bin roast an emu too in the stove! That emu your dreaming and my mother's [from] Bloods Creek and Charlotte Waters.

**Having 'bad luck'**

Death and associated rituals present another significant indirect reminder of traditional patterns of behaviour and belief. Word of someone's death spreads like wildfire through the whole community. Even when this occurs elsewhere a telephone call or telegram received by one person is very soon communicated to all in the town. There is no 'organisation' in a western sense as to how this will happen. No one specially undertakes the task. As people call at the shop and see each other in the street or visit the community centre, hospital, one another's homes, word passes from person to person in the random course of daily events.

When someone dies their relatives are referred to as 'having bad luck'. Even when recording information for a family tree people speaking of a death many years before use the same expression: 'so and so had bad luck with her son'. Almost the first information one is told on returning to Oodnadatta after an absence is who has had 'bad luck'. Since names are never mentioned and the word 'death' is never used it is all done indirectly by referring to so and so's husband, wife, son, granddaughter and so on.

Funerals themselves are western affairs today at least on the surface. The local cemetery is shared by all in the town and the services conducted by Aboriginal laypreachers from Coober Pedy. Older female relatives and one old man wail in a traditional manner once the coffin is lowered. Some close relatives cut their hair off nearly to the scalp and weep openly. All participants file past and place earth in the grave and then shake hands with a line of relatives and the preachers.

The name of a deceased person is not mentioned for some time following a death, as is common throughout Aboriginal Australia. Anyone with the same name as the deceased has to cease using that name. They may be known as *kunmanyi* or *minji* [motherless]. Today the term *wuni* is also used to describe a person holding the name of a deceased person. In the school records names are altered. One child listed as Michael Kim was later listed as Kim Michael. In this case his father with the same name had died and people were therefore calling him by his second name, Kim.

The senior women are probably the most correct in observing traditionally appropriate behaviour following a death. One woman was very upset to see a photograph of a recently deceased person inside a book of genealogies. General community permission had been given to include photographs of deceased people so they could be remembered by their descendants. She tore this photo from the book and ripped it up in my presence. Interestingly, no one else expressed any upset or concern over this photograph, which was of a group of people taken some time before that person's death.

**Family ties**

Another element of traditional behaviour upheld strongly by senior women is a respect for the right of each person or family group to speak for themselves. Women in particular are very conscious of this 'ownership' of knowledge. For instance, when recording family trees I would be referred directly to each family for information. It was clearly not considered correct behaviour to pass on someone else's genealogy unless they were present and willing to participate.

On one occasion we visited an old woman who was the last remaining person in her tribal group. We then visited the old woman's daughter to explain to her why we had called on her mother. This was to ensure that the daughter and her family would in turn not feel insulted.

In areas of traditional knowledge women referred us to senior men first, but concerning their own or their parents' Dreaming that is, their property, they were quite willing to share some knowledge. One woman who had left the area of her birth as a young child asked a man with more detailed knowledge of her birth place and 'Dreaming' to accompany us and provide further details she did not know. When he was not sufficiently forthcoming she insisted he tell all he knew, at times bullying him and joking him along.

Younger men and women defer to older siblings or relatives in their family over genealogical information. Such behaviour is courteous and deferential and aimed at minimising conflict and avoiding antagonism. It is based on premises very different from those which operate in the mainstream of Australian western society today, and resembles the eastern world's attitudes to seniority amongst both genders.

Conversely the senior women would become fierce and quite militant when someone did not recognise their rights and responsibilities. On one occasion two elderly women fought the Department of Community Welfare and a younger family member over custody of an orphaned grandchild. They are known within and without the community as formidable women. They have a reputation for fierceness in standing up for what they want. Traditionally this behaviour is appropriate and they command much respect (and sometimes exasperation too) among Aborigines and Europeans.

When I visited Oodnadatta with senior women who had moved away from the area, the middle-aged women greeted them with a handshake and a respectful welcome. The older women have always commented later that they like the woman who does this most consistently. It is clearly linked with her maintenance of these respectful forms.

The Aboriginal network of family provides a more workable practical extended support group for mothers with children than women receive in small nuclear families in the wider Australian society. It has already been noted how news of a death in the community spreads so swiftly. This is true of other significant personal information also. Births, illnesses, sexual relationships, quarrels, receipt of large amounts of money, movement from one location to another are all communicated swiftly and informally via a network of family and relatives. This is not without a certain amount of distortion, misinformation and conjecture.

In 1967 Buckley et al observed: 'It is noteworthy that many of the children we saw were being cared for by aunts, grandmothers or more distant kin. These children were not, in most cases, motherless, but their mothers were said to be sick, or to drink too heavily' (1967: 55). This pattern remains significant today. On every visit I observed one particular older woman who was childless, always had one or two of her younger sister's children in tow, nurturing and feeding them. Grandmothers would bring young grandchildren on bush trips lasting several days because the children were currently living with them. A man who had quarrelled with his brother was careful to explain the love and concern he had for his brother's children since they were like his own. These are examples of a widespread and supportive network of kinship ties which operate over a wide area in the north of South Australia.

Great suffering and loss was felt by children in the past when they were taken from their families and deprived of such family links. Their parents and relatives also suffered silently over long years. This loss has only recently been understood outside the community and documented (see Gibson, in press).

## Sustaining the role of women

It is in the minutiae of daily life, in the behaviour and attitudes which they reveal, that women's surviving cultural knowledge and the importance of their role in the Oodnadatta Aboriginal community is revealed.

Women in the Oodnadatta community today have significant and complementary roles to those of men. These are expressed through: their reaffirmation of links with traditional sites by visits whenever possible; their independent knowledge of cultural matters from a female point of view, which is however fast deteriorating; their important role in networks of kinship and the care of children; their moral custodianship of traditionally 'right' ways of behaviour; their continuing knowledge of some bush foods and how to find and prepare them; and their strength and balance in the difficult and often conflicting situations which life today brings.

Several of the women in their 30s and 40s are now assuming, or re-assuming, important roles in decision-making concerning the numerous ventures in which the Aboriginal community is involved today.

Marked changes have occurred internally to the Oodnadatta

township since the closure of the railway line in 1980, giving Aboriginal people a far greater degree of control of its facilities. Incorporated first as the Oodnadatta Aboriginal Housing Society and more recently as Danjibar Aboriginal Community, the community has acquired and renovated numerous railway houses, the town dam, the Transcontinental Hotel, the original general store and post office, and the railway station, which in December 1987 was opened as a museum. The post office, store and the hotel are managed by white employees selected by the Aboriginal people who also impose 8 pm closing on the hotel and limit bottle sales to beer only. In 1988 the community implemented a 'work for the dole' project.

Lack of interest amongst younger people is one of the reasons that traditional knowledge is lost. By appreciating and documenting such knowledge a positive attitude to traditional knowledge is encouraged. Bruce Shaw and I were employed as anthopologists/oral historians by the Oodnadatta Aboriginal people themselves, funded by the Commonwealth National Estate Grants Program. They were our bosses from 1985–1987. I felt comfortable and honoured, as an outsider, to be undertaking research at Oodnadatta with the purpose of promoting and recording the history of the people and their town through genealogies and life stories of some of the older women. This research is intended for local Oodnadatta use and benefit.

Many of the observations made here might be overlooked by someone living in the community. 'It is not possible to depend entirely upon what each nation says of its own habits of thought and action. . . Any country takes them for granted' (Benedict 1967: 10). There is need of both an inside and an outside point of view. These are both ways of recognising the value of Aboriginal women's traditional role and cultural knowledge. To appreciate the value of something and to make the participants feel positive about its worth is to sustain it despite ongoing changes. By so doing we enrich not only Australian society in general but world culture, for we are now all interconnected.

## References

Bell, D. (1983) *Daughters of the Dreaming*, Melbourne: McPhee Gribble/ George Allen & Unwin

Benedict, R. (1967) *The Chrysanthemum and the Sword* London: Routledge & Kegan Paul

Berndt R.M. and C.H. (1951) *From Black to White in South Australia* Cheshire, Melbourne

Berndt, C. H. (1965) 'Women and the secret life' in R.M. and C.H. Berndt (eds) *Aboriginal Man in Australia* Sydney: Angus & Robertson, pp. 238–282
Blackwell, D. and Lockwood, D. (1965) *Alice on the Line* Adelaide: Rigby
Buckley, R., Ellis, C.J., Hercus, L.A., Penny, L. and White, I.M. (1967) 'Group Project on Andagarinja Women' Vol 1 Adelaide: private publication, University of Adelaide Library
Buckley, R., Ellis, C.J., Hercus, L., and White, I.M. (1968) Group Project on Andagarinja Women' Vol 2 Adelaide: private publication, University of Adelaide Library
Cockburn, R. (1984) *What's in a name? Nomenclature of South Australia* Adelaide Ferguson
Elkin, A.P. (1931) 'Social Organisation of South Australian Tribes' *Oceania* 2, 1, pp. 44–73
Elkin, A.P. (1940) 'Kinship in South Australia' *Oceania* 10, 4 pp. 369–388
Gale, F. (1972) *Urban Aborigines* Canberra: Australian National University Press
Gibson, J. (1987) *Some Oodnadatta Genealogies* Adelaide: Aboriginal Heritage Branch, Department of Environment and Planning
—— (in press) *Molly Lennon's Story: That's how it was* Adelaide: Aboriginal Heritage Branch, Department of Environment and Planning
Hamilton, A. (1981) *Nature and Nurture. Aboriginal Child-rearing in north central Arnhem Land* Canberra: Australian Institute of Aboriginal Studies
Hercus, L. (1971) 'Arabana and Wangganguru Traditions' *Oceania*, 42, 2
Hercus, L. (1985) 'Leaving The Simpson Desert' *Aboriginal History* 9, 1 pp. 22–43
Howitt, A.W. (1891) 'The Dieri and other kindred tribes of Central Australia' *Journal of Anthropological Institute of Great Britain* pp. 30–105
Howitt, A.W. (1904) *Native tribes of south-east Australia* London: MacMillan
Johnson, C. (1983) *Doctor Wooreddy's Prescription for Enduring the Ending of the World* Melbourne: Hyland House
Montessori, M. (1948) *The Discovery of the Child* Madras: Kalakshetra
Morgan, S. (1987) *My Place* Fremantle: Fremantle Arts Centre Press
Reader, P. (1983) The heritage of the Antikirinya, Arabana and South Aranda land, unpublished report, Adelaide: Aboriginal Heritage Branch, Department of Environment and Planning
Second Kimberley Aboriginal women's meeting, report, Lake Gregory, 3–7 May 1985
Strehlow, T.G.H. (1947) *Aranda Traditions* Melbourne: Melbourne University Press
—— (1965) 'Culture, social structure and environment in Aboriginal Central Australia' in R.M. and C.H. Berndt (eds) *Aboriginal man in Australia* Sydney, pp. 121–145
White, I., Barwick, D. and Meehan, B eds (1985) *Fighters and Singers: the lives of some Australian Aboriginal women* Sydney: Allen and Unwin

# 5

# 'WOMEN TALKING UP BIG':
## Aboriginal women as cultural custodians, a South Australian example

### Jane M. Jacobs

As HAS already been suggested elsewhere in this volume, until recently the role of women in Aboriginal society, as custodians of an important and often exclusive body of cultural knowledge, has been ignored or downplayed. The increasing number of female researchers working with Aboriginal women in recent times has resulted in this imbalance slowly being redressed. The previous lack of understanding or acknowledgement of the knowledge and 'business' of Aboriginal women reflected a complex of gender relations and ideologies operating in the cross-cultural setting. On the one hand, Aboriginal women were ignored because the majority of research was conducted by men who transferred their gender biases to the Aboriginal realm. They assumed all religious and land-related knowledge to be the exclusive domain of Aboriginal men. On the other hand, male anthropologists were operating within the specific restrictions of Aboriginal society. As men they were denied access to the often secret and exclusively female realm of women's ceremonies and knowledge. The religion and Dreaming of men was often assumed to be the source of all spiritual life in the Aboriginal community. Women were viewed as 'profane', only participating in 'small-time' rituals and magic, not tied to the important issues of survival and the maintenance of harmony in the community and the environment (see, for example, Elkin, 1939; Kaberry, 1939; Maddock, 1974).

A growing enthnography now demonstrates that Aboriginal women do have an extensive and, some argue, autonomous cultural realm (see, for example, Bell, 1983b; Hamilton, 1981). Although it is important to consider the unique nature of Aboriginal women's knowledge in order to redress existing imbalances, it is also essential to highlight the nature of gender relations, both within the Aboriginal communities and cross-culturally, and how this influences the status of Aboriginal women's knowledge. This is important particularly in terms of the capacity of Aboriginal women to manage properly the knowledge over which they are custodians. The issue then is not so much whether a specific and exclusively or primarily female body of knowledge exists, this is now a widely acknowledged and increasingly documented aspect of Aboriginal culture. More important is the status of this knowledge within a framework of gender relations operating intrinsically (within the community), extrinsically (in dominant white society) and in the cross-cultural realm.

This paper will draw essentially on my own field experience of the past seven years in the Port Augusta/Flinders Ranges areas of South Australia. Firstly, the nature and status of cultural information over which women of this region are custodians will be overviewed. The 'status' of this knowledge is intrinsically linked to the power Aboriginal women have to manage their 'business' adequately and appropriately. Their custodianship, by necessity, now operates in a cross-cultural context. While they may continue to manage and maintain rituals, objects and sites within the community, they must also engage in the processes which ensure these sites are managed and maintained within the cross-cultural setting. Protecting sites from mining or other activities, ensuring a role in the consultation procedure and directing research, are all now part of the way in which Aboriginal women (and men) must ensure the safety and well-being of their culture. Thus a second theme of this paper is the increasingly important, but not unproblematic, relationship between Aboriginal women and official bodies, and with researchers given the responsibility of providing assistance to Aboriginal groups seeking to protect their cultural inheritance. Such official bodies include museums, research centres, site recording authorities as well as the independent researchers, whose activities often intersect with the cultural concerns of Aboriginal groups. Equally, funding bodies, through their financial support, often have the capacity to assist Aboriginal groups in the maintenance and in some cases the revival of cultural traditions.


## The field context

One of the reasons that male Aboriginal culture came to be seen as representing all Aboriginal culture was that male anthropologists who entered the field failed to acknowledge that their work operated within the limitations of their own gender biases as well as the gender restrictions within Aboriginal society. So too do white female researchers operate within certain limitations and expectations relating to both Aboriginal culture and their own cultural realm. I entered the field as a young, childless, white, female, postgraduate student and each of these labels influenced my experience and understanding of the communities with which I worked. Being female meant I had limited access to the business and knowledge of men. Being young and childless meant that my access to some realms of women's business and knowledge was also limited. All researchers, then, be they white or black, female or male, carry their own identity into the field with them and this acts to shape the picture created (cf Clifford, 1986; Bell 1983b). To acknowledge the cultural baggage one takes into research is the first step away from recreating the false picture of 'objectivity' painted by early white, male accounts of Aboriginal culture, which extrapolated the experience of all Aborigines from that of Aboriginal men.

For the most part I have worked in South Australia and, in particular, in and around the regional town centre of Port Augusta. The people I have worked with identify as Adnjama-thanha, those from the northern Flinders Ranges; Kukata, those from the area directly north west of Port Augusta; and Pangkala, those associated with the Gawler Ranges and eastern Eyre Peninsula. The Adnjamathanha are culturally and linguistically distinct, while there are considerable cultural and now political links between those who identify as Pangkala and Kukata. Although I have worked specifically with these groups and in the aforementioned places, I have also collected information relating to other parts of South Australia and in particular areas further north and west. The bulk of my work has related to Aboriginal land rights efforts and the theme of post-contact relationships with the land (Jacobs, 1983, 1985, 1988, Press). Other research was completed with Caroline Laurence and Faith Thomas on an oral and archival history of one of the missions in the area (Jacobs, Laurence and

Thomas, in press). In addition to my South Australian experience I
have worked extensively on rock art sites throughout Australia.
This work was undertaken in conjunction with Professor Fay Gale
of the Department of Geography, University of Adelaide, around
the theme of visitor impact on and responses to Aboriginal rock art
sites (Gale and Jacobs, 1987).

My own field work did not seek to explore gender relations
explicitly but it was unavoidable that this became a consideration.
This in part reflects the importance of gender-specific knowledge
and roles in Aboriginal society. Thus a researcher such as myself
who is female is logically more involved with Aboriginal women
and their specific concerns and 'business'. However, the emphasis
on gender in my own research, as with that of others, also reflects a
more general awareness in academic and popular thinking that
gender and gender relations affect the relative power and status of
men and women within a society (cf Connell, 1987).

In the research I have undertaken in the Port Augusta region
the emphasis has been on Aboriginal groups perceived by outsiders
to be 'non-traditional' or 'semi-traditional'. Such groups have
suffered greatly in the loss of traditional knowledge and practices
due to contact. Because of this they had been largely ignored by anthropologists and other researchers, who for many years worked
with more overtly traditional groups and used the ethnographic
material to reconstruct Aboriginal culture as it might have been in
its pristine pre-contact state. Thus these 'non-traditional' groups
not only faced the erosion of traditional practices and knowledge
due to contact, they were often denied researchers' interest in
recording or retrieving what was left of a diminishing but still
vibrant body of traditional knowledge (although many from this
area feel that the lack of interest from researchers has in some ways
been an advantage). Furthermore, the emphasis on reconstruction
of a pristine pre-contact world has meant many important processes of change and adaptation of traditional knowledge and
customary practices were for many years virtually ignored. It is
within this context that I chose to work in the town of Port Augusta
and surrounding areas.

## The changing status of women's land-related
## 'business' in anthropological writing

It is often hard to disentangle the internal status of Aboriginal
women's 'business' among tradition-orientated groups and the
status given it by analysts who work within their own changing

cultural and theoretical traditions. While the contact experience
has wrought real changes to the status and power of Aboriginal
women (and men), much of the research into the status of women
in tradition-orientated groups has been transformed by theoretical
considerations often quite external to Aboriginal society. The
'changing status' of Aboriginal women's 'business' must, in part, be
viewed in the context of the shifting views on the role and status of
women within dominant Australian society, and the projection of
these ideas onto Aboriginal society (cf Clifford and Marcus, 1986).
Since it was acknowledged that Aboriginal women do more than
'feed' and 'breed', the way the status and role of women within
Aboriginal society has been interpreted has changed. This change
is tied both to improved access to this information (researchers
started to talk to Aboriginal women) and, an interrelated factor,
the changing theorising of gender relations in academic circles.
Thus while Kaberry's (1939) work, and that of Goodale published
much later (1971), did much to elucidate the existence of a specific
realm of ritual and ceremonial knowledge among women, they still
concluded that this knowledge was somehow less important than
that held by men. The lower status of women was reflected in the
fact they were largely excluded from what was then interpreted by
anthropologists to be the ceremony of ceremonies, male initiation.
Elkin's introduction to Kaberry (1939) made this point clear,
despite his earlier encouragement of research focusing on Aboriginal women (cf Elkin, 1935). Marie Reay's much later overview of
research into Aboriginal women, although also promoting the
need to study Aboriginal women, casually noted that in desert
areas '. . . the men have a full rich and interesting secret life, and
the women have a few scrappy little ceremonies of their own'
(1963:326). This view would be hotly contested by some researchers, not to mention the Aboriginal women (see, for example, Bell
1983b; Hamilton, 1981).

    Other female anthropologists perpetuated Kaberry's model in
which women were seen as partly independent but still subservient
to the male order. Analysts such as Isobel White (1974) argued that
because women married older men they were the 'junior partners'
and that in all spheres of Aboriginal life their status was below that
of men. The existence of a separate, female ceremonial sphere was
acknowledged but it was seen to be less important than that of men
because it was supposedly inward-looking, dealing with issues of
particular concern to women rather than society as a whole. In
contrast the ceremonies of men were interpreted as more important because they purportedly dealt with issues concerning all of
society. Bell (1983b:244) describes this phase of the analysis as the

'anthropology of women', in which the *role* of women in Aboriginal society was highlighted but their *status* was not reinterpreted. More was uncovered about Aboriginal women, but this did not alter the way their status in Aboriginal society was understood by researchers. Bell correctly notes that the analysis of the status of women in Aboriginal society was still being constrained by the gender models current in western thinking. Further, the analysis of women of terms of their *roles* within Aboriginal society failed to come to grips with their relative *power*, a factor crucial to any understanding of status.

There has been little agreement among anthropologists regarding the status of Aboriginal women in traditional society. While White proposed a 'junior partner' explanation, Catherine Berndt formulated an alternate model of gender relations, based on her own extensive field work. At the 1969 ANZAAS Conference (the proceedings of which are published in Gale, 1978) Berndt presented her 'two-sex model' of gender relations in Aboriginal society which posited an 'interdependent independence' of the sexes. She implied that men and women had separate roles which were different and complementary. This more balanced interpretation of gender relations in Aboriginal society was seen to be most apparent in the economic sphere but least apparent in the ceremonial sphere in which, Berndt argued, women participated but only to a limited extent. Berndt has also been instrumental in resisting simplified interpretations of the status of Aboriginal women. In her commentary on Marie Reay's paper at the 1961 AIAS Conference, she stressed that the status of Aboriginal women is 'multi-faceted', varying with age, child-bearing, ownership of rites and even personality (Berndt, 1963; 340)

Catherine Berndt's perspective is indicative of what seems to be a general resistance among more recent anthropologists to the cross-cultural application of a 'universalist' view of women as subordinate to men. This is apparent even among some of the most recent work drawing explicitly on a feminist perspective. Hester Eisenstein (1984; 132) noted that in many cases the emergence of a feminist analysis of women's status 'in spite of its narrow base of white, middle-class experience, purported to speak about and on behalf of all women, black or white, poor or rich'. Contrary to this, in the main currents of feminist analysis of Aboriginal women there has been acknowledgement that female subordination is not clear cut and in some spheres of life is quite inaccurate. Rather there is an attempt to 'seek the origins and mechanisms by which gender hierarchies and such cultural dogmas as sexual asymmetry are established and maintained' (Bell, 1983b; 244). This type of

perspective not only shifts the view of gender relations in traditional Aboriginal society away from the 'universalist' application of
a model of female subordination but also away from the romantic
search for sexual egalitarianism in Aboriginal, and all hunter-
gatherer, societies.

The most recent chapter in the ongoing analysis and re-
evaluation of the status of women in Aboriginal society is still
fraught with divergent views regarding the status of Aboriginal
women in tradition-orientated Aboriginal society. For example, Di
Bell's extensive ethnography of the Kaytej and Warlpiri women of
Central Australia presents one strand of the most recent thought.
Bell's essential concern is the nature and status of women's
knowledge, but not from the point of view of how this is perceived
by outsiders or by men within the group. Her prime and distinguishing interest is in how Aboriginal women *themselves* see their
role and status within their society. After an extensive and in-depth
period of participating in the ceremonial life of the Kaytej, Bell
presented an analysis of these women as powerful, independent,
autonomous members of their society, responsible for ceremonial
matters essential for the continued well-being of the entire social
group and the land. She concludes that women have a 'vital and
complementary role' in maintaining the *jukurrpa* heritage (Dreaming) and that 'it is through the co-operative endeavours of both
men and women that the *jukurrpa* is maintained' (Bell, 1983b;
230).

A complementary but divergent view is presented by Annette
Hamilton, drawing on her experience in both central and northern
Australia (Hamilton, 1975, 1981) Unlike Bell, Hamilton is explicitly concerned with the realm of gender relations and relative
power: how men see women, how women see men as well as how
they see themselves. Hamilton (1975) stresses that Aboriginal
women are the basic 'means of production' in traditional groups
and as such are 'objects'. Shifting somewhat from her earlier
position she argues (1981) that there is not a clear picture of female
subordination in traditional Aboriginal society and stresses that
they have an autonomous economic and social life. She remains
committed to there being a 'definite asymmetry' in gender
relations which 'elaborates an ideology of male superiority and
maintains that superiority by excluding women' (1981: 81). But she
places this within a context which elaborates the notion of power.
For Hamilton, then, the question is this: 'which sex is the more
powerful, in which context, and how is the pattern of those power
relations maintained, reproduced, and sometimes transcended?'

(1981: 74). The importance of this question is that it suggests that power for Aboriginal women is variable and contingent. In some spheres and in some situations they are more powerful than others. This is far closer to the practice-based theory of gender relations proposed by Connell, for example, which concerns itself with understanding the 'interweaving of personal lives and social structures' (1987: 351).

The changing analysis of the status of women in traditional Aboriginal society, and particularly in relation to their traditional, land-related 'business', reflects shifting or developing notions of gender relations in academic circles as much as the reality of Aboriginal society. Although Berndt, Bell and Hamilton have paid particular attention to how traditional status has been modified and eroded by changes wrought by contact, the debates have failed to address issues relating to less traditional groups where customary patterns of gender relations have long gone or have been greatly influenced by the patterns imposed by the dominant white society.

## The nature of women's knowledge in the study area

From my varied field work there are two themes of particular relevance to this paper. Firstly, women's knowledge of mythology and ceremony relating to social relations and the land and, secondly, women's knowledge about contact experiences and family history. In both cases the concern is with how these two aspects of the lives of Aboriginal women in the Port Augusta region shape their status within the community and in the cross-cultural realm. This is not to suggest that these are the only issues about which Aboriginal women in this area are knowledgeable. On the contrary, they have many other areas of expertise such as knowledge about food and medicines, childcare, song, and arts and crafts, to name but a few.

What constitutes the body of information over which women are custodians in part reflects the varying roles they hold or have held within the community. These roles have changed dramatically since contact and consequently the expertise or realm of knowledge of women has also changed. This is particularly so in the area around Port Augusta, where Aborigines have suffered massive disruption due to contact. Pastoral activities, missions (like Nepabunna in the Flinders Ranges, Koonibba to the west, Umeewarra children's home in Port Augusta and Colebrook children's home at

Quorn), the laying of the east-west railwayline and the later incursion of mining, have made for intensive disruption of Aboriginal life in this area. The regional centre of Port Augusta has long operated as a focus for Aboriginal migration, attracting Aborigines from all parts of the State, but particularly the north and the west. Thus in the Port Augusta region there is an enormous range of women not only from different tribal groups, but also women with different contact experiences, and different configurations of 'knowledge' relating to both traditional culture and the contact experience.

While some women may lack a knowledge of the Dreaming or ceremony, they may hold valuable information relating to family history or contact experiences. It is a reflection of the imposition of our own judgements about what constitutes authentic and valuable knowledge in Aboriginal society that for many years the contact experience had been relegated to the sidelines of our enquiries into Aboriginal culture. This is reflected in the way in which Aborigines often relate to researchers. Under the impression that, like most other researchers, I was only interested in traditional business, Aboriginal women would often strain to provide me with vaguely remembered snippets of mythologies. Yet on the topic of ration distribution, early relations with the police, medical provision under the Protector of Aborigines, or growing up or managing a family on a mission, they were able to draw on a rich body of personal and community experience.

In many cases there is a residual knowledge of ways and beliefs which no longer necessarily play an essential part in day to day survival but which now have a prime role in the long-term cultural and political survival of Aboriginal identity. Depending on the contact experiences of particular groups and individuals, knowledge of traditional matters will vary. In the Port Augusta region some women still participate in ritual activity, others have only what their mothers (or others) told them, never having actively participated in ceremonies designed to teach and maintain such knowledge. Others feel that because the old ways are gone they cannot safely or rightfully involve themselves in this side of Aboriginal culture.

My work with Aboriginal women in Port Augusta revealed that there is a small group of women who still hold close connections with more tradition-orientated groups further north, and have an extensive and varied knowledge of song cycles, mythologies and associated rituals. These relate to the maintenance of the land and survival (including menstruation, childbirth, ageing, plant and animal species and practices of exploiting and maintaining the natural environment). Many of the ceremonial activities of women are based around appeasing or regulating social disharmony or suffering, both for the self and for relatives. These activities include the maintenance of harmonious social relations within the community, the resolution of conflict or grief, and the teaching of cultural and social laws. Research into female ceremonies in other parts of Australia has shown this to be a major emphasis of women's 'business'. Bell (1983b), for examples produces a large body of evidence which suggests Aboriginal women are in control of an autonomous body of knowledge related to the management of social relations and the nurturance and regeneration of the land.

The nurturing and regenerative theme of women's ceremonial activity is clearly important and can confer much status within the community on those women who actively participate in such activities. In the Port Augusta region most women who participate in such activities live on Davenport Reserve or spend much of their time there. Some have chosen to live away from the reserve in town (either Port Augusta or Whyalla) so as to avoid the frequent conflicts, the drinking or the pressures to lend money, but still spend some of their time at Davenport with other women talking 'business' or catching up on gossip. These older women of Davenport are respected in the wider Aboriginal community (including Port Augusta and Whyalla) as women who have been able to go on caring for the Dreaming and the land. When these women sing for the country they are seen as, and see themselves as, singing for all Aboriginal women in the area. Occasionally, less knowledgeable women from the same or related tribal groups will seek advice from these older women or their relatives in the north. Indeed, among some groups whose cultural traditions had suffered erosion since contact, there was a growing link with more tradi-tional groups further north. The Kukata, for example, regularly sought assistance and advice over land matters from the Pitjantjat-jara whose knowledge of the land was often seen as stronger than that of the Kukata people. The Pitjantjatjara elders have been able to confirm matters for the Kukata in the absence of their own group of elders.

Other women in the Port Augusta region know simplified versions of these stories but have only a partial or non-existent knowledge of the associated songs and rituals. Often the storyline may be known and spoken in its Aboriginal version but many mythologies are now known and told only in English. This variety in the degrees of knowledge is also apparent among men in this area. It does not in any way reflect on the importance of such information to women in the Port Augusta region. Knowledge

about the Dreaming which is still embedded in its traditional
context of language and ceremony is no more or less important
than an abbreviated version of the same mythology known only in
English. Each is seen as a valuable cultural inheritance to be
protected and maintained.

## Women as custodians of land-based knowledge in the cross-cultural setting

An important issue associated with the contemporary custodianship of traditional, land-related knowledge is the recording of this
information either by outside agencies which seek to confer legal
protection on the sites or by researchers (be they whites or
members of the Aboriginal community) seeking to record such
information for cultural 'posterity'. The pressure to record such
information is now intense as it is realised that oral traditions are
being eroded and that recorded versions of traditional culture
carry enormous cultural and political value in issues relating to
land rights.

In this context of the shift towards recording cultural information, both by outsiders and by Aboriginal communities, the
willingness of women (and, indeed, men) to communicate such
information both to others within their tribal group or community
and to outsiders, such as researchers, is a major issue. In many ways
the willingness of Aboriginal women to pass on cultural information for recording reflects both the nature of gender relations
within these groups, the status of women's knowledge and the
power Aboriginal women have regarding the management of their
'business'. More than any other knowledge, it is information
associated with the Dreaming which has, and remains subject to,
gender specific controls regarding access and dissemination. These
controls reflect to a large extent internally held values but also, in
areas like Port Augusta, the impact of external influences.

Those women, well-versed in knowledge and ceremony which is
their exclusive domain, actively protect the often secret and
autonomous status of this knowledge and their role as custodians.
When appropriate, ceremonies are conducted away from the main
community, and more specifically, away from male members of the
community. In the Port Augusta region most women who actively
participate in such ceremony live at Davenport Reserve, on the
fringe of the main town. In such an environment it is often difficult
for them to arrange the privacy necessary for the performance of
certain ceremonies. Many only participate in such activities infre-

quently, when they make visits to family in the north, for example. Women who have such an active knowledge of the Dreaming are faced with all the customary limits and obligations with regard to passing this information on to less knowledgeable women within their own groups or to outsiders.

Women who have a less complete or active knowledge of the Dreaming have different restrictions and inhibitions relating to their ability to communicate this knowledge. Often the knowledge they have was passed on to them outside of the customary setting of ceremony. Perhaps it was told to them in confidence by their mother or an aunt. Perhaps the family lived on a mission where such information was frowned upon by the missionary. A combination of factors tends to make most women with only a partial knowledge of the Dreaming very reluctant to pass on or record what they know. In many cases this arises out of the women's uncertainty as to their right to know such information, let alone pass it on. These women then are custodians of information but are not, because of the breakdown in their traditional ways, entirely cognisant with the correct procedures by which to manage this information. Many feel that they can only communicate such information in the company of other older women (even if these women do not know the story being discussed), others fear that they would be talking out of turn and they might get into trouble with other more knowledgeable women, some may know the sites associated with the story but are reluctant to visit them because they are unsure of the full implications of doing so. At the same time these women are well aware of the need to ensure that Aboriginal culture survives and their children grow up with knowledge of and pride in their Aboriginal heritage. All these pressures play on Aboriginal women who are custodians of what remains of their traditional culture. The relationship between Aboriginal women and external agents will be shaped, in part, by the dilemmas that face these women. External agencies and researchers are currently the main source of the skill needed to record such information and there is often a sense of obligation among women to pass over information in order to ensure it is recorded and thereby protected under white law. One of the notable products of assisting Aboriginal women with undertaking their own research and recording of cultural information is that these dilemmas can be resolved internally and with the minimum of external pressure.

Thus far I have discussed the pressures facing Aboriginal women who are knowledgeable about matters relating to Dreaming and ceremonies which are traditionally the exclusive responsibility of women, that is, it is their 'business' to be managed as they see fit. In many communities and especially in the Port Augusta region this gender division of knowledge has been blurred as a result of changes through contact. Some women, for example, know of mythological cycles but are unsure if they are 'men's business', 'women's business' or open. This means they are very cautious about how they deal with this information in case they are inadvertantly meddling in 'men's business' and thereby breaching customary practice.

A more complex example of this blurring of the gender division of knowledge arises from a situation where women might know information about traditionally exclusive male mythologies and practices from male members of the family. Such women have the unenviable responsibility of being the custodians of information which, under customary law, they should not know. Often they are one of the few remaining people who have this knowledge. In such circumstances there is often pressure from younger members of the community and outsiders for such women to pass on this information or to have it recorded in some way. This places them in a most difficult position. To pass on such information would be a breach of customary laws relating to women discussing 'men's business'. Further, the very fact that some women are custodians of such knowledge reflects on the male member of the group who, in passing this information on, is also seen as not having complied with gender-based rules of secrecy, despite there being evidence to suggest that over time gender-specific song-cycles can become open. Added to these pressures are usually fears that what is known is only fragmentary and may not be accurate. The dilemma of these women reflects the more general difficulty facing women who are aware of information and yet are not certain as to the cultural obligations associated with this knowledge, and who must confront the pressures from within and without to record what remains of their traditional culture.

Both Bell (1983b) and Hamilton (1981) stress the impact of the erosion of women's land-based activities, both economic and spiritual, on their loss of status and the shift from female autonomy to male dominance and to women's dependence on men. Certainly in the Port Augusta region both economic and spiritual aspects of land association have been seriously eroded for most women. They have also been seriously eroded for men, although their work as stockmen often provided opportunities for the *in situ* passing on of information about the land. But it is not only that there may be a real difference in the amount of land-based knowledge and activity retained by men and women in this region. Within the Aboriginal communities in the area there has also been a growing ascendency of the ideology that men have the only valuable and worthwhile land-based 'business'.

The title of this paper, 'women talking up big', is an adaptation of a comment once made by an Aboriginal man in Port Augusta about a group of women talking about land-related matters. His version was, 'these women talk up too big'. In the Port Augusta region it is common for men to be angered by the women being given special attention by researchers. They are happy for the women to discuss certain issues, such as those relating to family or traditional food sources, but find it more difficult to accept that women have knowledge about, and a right to discuss, matters relating to mythology and the land. I do not have first hand knowledge of the nature of gender relations in other more tradition-oriented communities, but gather from Bell's work (1983a, 1983b) that the entire community accepts that women have a separate and autonomous sphere of ritual and ceremony associated with the land. The emergence of women's councils in many other communities suggests that elsewhere it is acknowledged that women have their own 'business' and own land-based concerns.

Why then the resistance and opposition among men in the Port Augusta region to women discussing land-related matters? This response by Aboriginal men to women talking about traditional matters and particularly matters relating to mythology and sites was especially apparent with regard to women who were known, or thought to have, a fragmented or partial knowledge of land-based 'business'. Often such censure came from men who themselves had no more complete knowledge about the land and associated rituals than did the women they censured. To a limited degree this reflects the same dilemma that faced Aboriginal women who were unsure of the appropriateness of discussing certain matters. In a context of a limited, sporadic and often no longer existent ceremonial life, men can also be unsure about the rights of individuals to speak out over certain issues. In this context of uncertainty regarding rights and responsibilities over traditional knowledge other, often external, notions about gender-based rights and responsibilities have become dominant. For example, a major factor in the dominance of Aboriginal men in land-related 'business' in the cross-cultural realm has been the bias of researchers towards men's interests in land. As a consequence when there was initial consultation regarding land matters (by government agencies, for example) it was the interests of men which received attention. Their mythologies, their sites and their ceremonies were all important and the landscape recorded was a male landscape and not a female one, a male culture not a female one. Thus the bias was not only reflected in publications or official records, it has been embedded in the consultation process. The result is that men are seen and, after years of acting as the main spokespeople on land matters, now often see themselves as bosses of such matters when discussed in the cross-cultural realm.

It is not surprising then that the public front of land rights politics in the Port Augusta region has been dominated by men rather than women. Although women often played a crucial behind-the-scenes role in administration and organisation of land rights efforts in the early 1980s in this region, all important discussions between the land rights groups and outsiders were conducted by men. It is also not surprising that when Aboriginal women in the Port Augusta region began to speak out about land issues they faced opposition and censure from the men who saw themselves, partly because of the way we have constructed their role, as having the right to control what women said about land matters. Indeed the entry of land issues which are the specific concern of women into the political realm has had a direct impact on the internal and cross-cultural political status held by Aboriginal men. Many Aboriginal men have been reluctant to forego the monopoly they have gained on land-related matters in the cross cultural realm (cf Jacobs, 1988, press).

This leads to a final point I would like to make in relation to the traditional, land-based knowledge of Aboriginal women. It is an issue which relates to recent developments in Australia (including South Australia) in which site recording authorities and related agencies like National Parks are likely to play an increasingly important role: the interpretation of sites for the general touring public. The new tourist development proposals for the Flinders Ranges are obviously of immediate concern for the Aborigines in the Port Augusta and Flinders Ranges areas. Within this context of tourist development the general issues of site protection and management become essential concerns (see Gale and Jacobs, 1987). But what of Aboriginal women in this context and what of their sites or sites which have some cultural content relating to women? In the work Fay Gale and I have undertaken on Aboriginal rock art sites we gave considerable attention to the interpretation of Aboriginal culture provided by 'official' guides and the attitudes of tourists to sites and to Aborigines in general. Two main points emerged which should be of immediate concern to Aboriginal women and to agencies involved in assisting Aboriginal groups with recording and protecting Aboriginal culture in the light of proposed tourist developments. First, tour guides tend to reinforce rather than challenge pre-existing views of Aboriginal culture in their interpretive talks. The vast majority see Aboriginal culture as male dominated. Of the various stereotypes portrayed, those of Aboriginal women are the most insidious and inaccurate. Those tour guides who discussed Aboriginal women (and many ignored them entirely), repeatedly portrayed them as little more than drudges and sex objects. Tourists too come with similar misconceptions about Aboriginal culture. They rarely see women as important members of Aboriginal society and assume that all art sites and mythological sites are men's sites.

The decision about which sites are opened to the public and how these sites are interpreted is a matter which ultimately should rest with the Aboriginal custodians. But in the light of increasing tourist development in Australia it is likely that Aboriginal communities and goverment agencies alike will have to confront the need to provide tourists with some form of interpretive information. These decisions need to be made with an understand-ing of how the general public is misconstruing Aboriginal culture and particularly the role and status of women in Aboriginal society.

## The contact experience and the historicity
## of gender relations

Thus far the discussion has focused on ceremonial and traditional land-based knowledge of Aboriginal women. Another important body of knowledge is that relating to experiences and memories of the contact period and family history. In recent years Aboriginal and white researchers alike have placed more emphasis on record-ing genealogies, family and community histories, memories of mission experiences, of living on rations and so on (see, for example, Lamilami, 1974; Shaw and McDonald, 1978; White et al 1985). Such oral and community history projects are exemplary and demonstrate the need to adopt a broad approach to the recording of cultural information. For most Aboriginal people it is not only traditional or customary knowledge which constitutes their unique sense of identity. It is also the history—often painful—of the destruction of this heritage and the formation of new, shared experiences during the period of contact. The contact experience is as much a part of contemporary Aboriginal culture as is the Dreaming. The experiences of resistance, of forced com-pliance, and of voluntary accommodation to white Australia all form part of Aboriginal identity and have played a major role in

shaping gender relations both within Aboriginal society and cross-
culturally. It is through an understanding of the contact experiences of Aboriginal women that it is possible to understand what
Connell (1987, 63) refers to as the 'historicity of gender': that is,
how gender relations have been transformed through the contact
experience.

Many of the Aboriginal women in Port Augusta are far more
confident and comfortable discussing aspects of Aboriginal culture
relating to family history and contact experiences than they are
discussing information on more traditional matters. In this area, as
in other parts of Australia, the economic and spiritual roles of
Aboriginal women (and men) were dramatically transformed by
the intrusion of white settlers. Aborigines fast became dependent
on rations and women became economically dependent on men.
They settled on pastoral leases or, more often, missions. Women
were, to a greater extent than men who had the option of working
in the pastoral industry, often tied to the mission settlements. This
disrupted their visits to their country and their performance of
rituals to maintain the country. Their role as educators of children
was undermined by mission activities, and they no longer directly
managed the health of their families. These changes substantially
eroded their traditional sources of status and power within their
own society. Women were left to run the family as best they could
within a context of often constant intervention of white officials
and missionaries, while the men were away working on pastoral
leases, railways or roads. They therefore have first hand experience of the impact on their lives of the varying government policies
towards Aborigines: from segregation, to assimilation, to self-
determination. One obvious and dramatic example of the impact
of government and mission intervention is the removal of children
from their mothers. The devastating effect on the mother as well
as the child, who was then usually placed into a mission or foster
home, has only just begun to be explored. Much of the most
poignant documentation of this period comes from the Aboriginal
women whose lives have been forever shaped by this tragic process.

Many of the Aboriginal women in the Port Augusta area have
lived through all or some of these phases of government policy.
Indeed, in the Port Augusta area the implementation of certain
policies was achieved by the incorporation of Aboriginal women,
well before men, in the various agencies providing services to the
Aboriginal community. The mission activities in the area, on the
one hand, worked to destroy traditional Aboriginal culture but, on
the other hand, provided the education needed to produce the first
Aboriginal nurses, teachers or welfare workers, most of whom

were women. Many of these women have now gone on to become leaders, both respected within their community and playing an important part in ensuring rights for Aboriginal people. Thus, while Aboriginal women have lost status in relation to their traditional land-based knowledge, some at least have gained a different status which is tied more closely to their roles within the cross-cultural sphere. That these opportunities appeared in these areas of Aboriginal affairs in part reflects white views of the sorts of jobs women do well.

That the contact experiences of Aboriginal culture have been, until recently, underplayed by researchers is largely a reflection of the biases of early anthropological research towards cultural reconstruction. Indeed many Aborigines in the Port Augusta region assume that white researchers are interested only in traditional matters. For example, when I first began work in the Port Augusta region I went to see a woman who I had been told had lived on a number of the camps on the outskirts of Port Augusta during the 1940s and 1950s. When I asked if she would work with me she immediately said she knew 'nothing' and that I should talk to one of the older women. In part this was the usual ploy to get rid of yet another white intruder. However a later trip around the edge of town with this woman revealed that she indeed was an expert on these camps and could not only tell me where they were but who lived there and what life was like. She thought she knew 'nothing' because she assumed I was interested only in the 'old days' and not in her time. But the sense among some of the women in Port Augusta that they know 'nothing' runs deeper than this example. It is not only thinking that they know 'nothing' but that what they do know is not of any value, again a reflection of previous biases in the way we have consulted with Aboriginal communities through the men and about particular aspects of Aboriginal society only.

Part of my involvement with the Aboriginal community of Port Augusta has been in the running of Family History and Genealogy workshops. The workshops were designed to teach Aboriginal people the skills needed to undertake research themselves. Aboriginal women were particularly important in this project and although family history is not a matter exclusively of interest to women, they are commonly accepted as, and see themselves to be, experts on family issues and the custodians of this sort of knowledge (Jacobs, 1985). The family history workshops did a great deal to reinstate the status of women's knowledge about family and life history. In these workshops the women were the experts. They knew who was born when and to whom. They knew what family life was like in the 1940s, for example. The workshops helped them to realise that the knowledge which they always carried with them was important, worth recording and had a significance for Aboriginal culture now and in the future as a record of resistance and survival.

### Consulting with aboriginal women—the future

The first step in the process of redressing the current gender imbalances outlined in this paper is to begin consulting with women and giving women particular attention in research. This is a process which is well under way. It is also important that the emergence of this emphasis is set within the broader question of gender relations in Aboriginal communities and in the cross-cultural realm. Consulting with Aboriginal women about issues expressly related to their interests and their sphere of knowledge requires an approach which accommodates the current responsibilities women have within the family and the community. There should also be an awareness of other community implications arising for women because of their involvement in a research project.

In a town like Port Augusta the Aboriginal women have the prime responsibility for raising the children, providing meals, and the general management of the household and family (making sure children get off to school, bills are paid etc.). In the Port Augusta area some women share their time between these responsibilities and those of full or part-time employment (often in a government department dealing specifically with Aboriginal issues). For these women it is often difficult to find time to commit to other matters. Simply getting to a land rights meeting was a major difficulty for some women, let alone being able to make regular visits to the country over which they hold a sense of responsibility. Often a night time meeting about land may follow a day of meetings at work. If attending a meeting was difficult, then going on a field trip was a major commitment of time and entailed general reorganisation of the family. It was necessary to make arrangements with relatives about caring for children, to get time off work, to ensure that payments got through and so on. Some of the more knowledgeable women on traditional matters are now quite old. They may not be encumbered by broader family responsibilities but may have limited mobility or particular health problems limiting their capacity to go on long trips or get into and out of a four-wheel drive. Thus there are very particular logistical problems related to arranging for a group of women to get together and go out into the field. The women need plenty of time to arrange who can go, when they can go and who will look after the family when they are gone. The various responsibilities facing women in the Port Augusta region means lengthy field trips are often impossible.

The reinstatement of the rightful status of Aboriginal women's 'business' in the cross-cultural realm also requires a policy commitment from relevant agencies. It is essential that official policy overtly expresses a commitment to the redressing of gender imbalances in programmes designed to assist Aborigines manage and maintain cultural matters. In the first instance this can be achieved by establishing programmes which specifically respond to the needs and interests of Aboriginal women. Once instituted in policy, certain 'structural' or administrative changes are necessary in the consultation procedure. The obvious solution is to have more women (white and Aboriginal) participating in the research process. At the official level this means more women employed as researchers, thereby ensuring that Aboriginal women are not denied the opportunity to work with a female anthropologist, historian, archaeologist or whatever the professional required. At the community level changes might also be required to ensure that women regain a sense of responsibility for and pride in their knowledge of Aboriginal culture. It has been demonstrated in many communities that the establishment of women's councils provides Aboriginal women with a mechanism through which their interests can be heard and acted upon. Such formal organisations also provide outside consultants with an appropriate and internally ratified point of contact with the Aboriginal women. They also provide the Aboriginal women with an official forum through which they can regulate the sort of research undertaken. As with all issues, it is up to the community to decide on the appropriateness of such councils or committees and the way in which they should be run. Indeed in the Port Augusta region such committees may have problems which do not face similar organisations in more culturally homogeneous communities.

Providing Aboriginal women with more resources and establishing mechanisms by which they might better protect their seriously eroded land interests is but a start. It is essential that the understanding of the status of Aboriginal women be set squarely within the context of gender relations. As this paper has suggested, the status of Aboriginal women and in particular their status in relation to land-based 'business' has changed dramatically in this area since contact. So too has the status of women changed in relation to matters relevant to the well-being of the family. While at one level they have lost considerable control over the daily maintenance of health and education in the family, at another level, some women, by way of their entrance into government agencies, have ensured these agencies will better meet the needs of their Aboriginal clients. Nevertheless the status of women in Aboriginal society is always contingent and changing with circumstances and with the purpose at hand.

As a closing point I would like to raise an issue which relates not only to Aboriginal women but to men as well. Much of the research involved in the recording of Aboriginal culture requires the presence of professionals, capable of recording sites and so on. But it cannot be overstated that the experts in Aboriginal culture are Aborigines themselves and that they are able to take on the responsibilities not only of deciding what sort of research is important to undertake but, increasingly, of doing the research themselves. Every effort should be made to break down the researcher/informant relationship which carries with it such complex and inequitable power relations. Many of the Aboriginal women I worked with through the family history workshops were not only keen to undertake research but were more than capable of doing so. This is not simply a process of employing or funding more Aborigines, although that is a fundamental element. It is now time for white researchers to open up about *their* knowledge of Aboriginal culture and actively ensure that Aborigines have the skills and resources needed to gain access to and re-evaluate the vast amounts of information we have appropriated and stored in museums and libraries in the past. It is the turn of white researchers to demystify and relinquish our positions as so-called 'experts' on Aboriginal culture.

Through these changes to policy and the mechanisms of consultation, and through the reinstatement of status and power in relation to the management and maintenance of cultural matters, it may be possible for Aboriginal women to once again 'talk up big'.

**References**

Bell, D. and Ditton, P. (1980) *Law: The Old and the New: Aboriginal Women in Central Australia Speak Out* Canberra: Aboriginal history for the Central Australian Aboriginal Legal Aid Service
Bell, D. (1983a) 'Consulting with women' in F. Gale (ed.) *We are Bosses Ourselves: The Role and Status of Aboriginal Women Today* Canberra: Australian Institute of Aboriginal Studies, pp. 24–8
Bell, D. (1983b) *Daughters of the Dreaming* Melbourne: McPee Gribble/ George Allen and Unwin

Berndt, C. (1963) 'Commentary' in H. Sheils (ed.) *Australian Aboriginal Studies* Melbourne: Oxford University Press, pp. 335–342
— (1970) Digging sticks and spears, or, the two-sex model' in F. Gale (ed.) *Woman's Role in Aboriginal Society* Canberra: Australian Institute of Aboriginal Studies, pp. 39–48
Clifford, J. (1986) 'Partial Truths' in J. Clifford and G. E. Marcus (eds) *Writing Culture: The Poetics and Politics of Ethnography* Berkeley: University of California Press
Clifford, J. and Marcus, G.E. eds (1986) *Writing Culture: The Poetics and Politics of Ethnography* Berkeley: University of California Press
Collmann J. (1988) ' "I'm a Proper Number One Fighter, Me": Aborigines, Gender, and Bureaucracy in Central Australia' in *Gender and Society* 2, 1 pp 9–23
Connell, R.W. (1987) *Gender and Power: Society, the Person and Sexual Politics* Oxford: Polity Press
Eisenstein, H. (1984) *Contemporary Feminist Thought* London: Unwin Paperbacks
Elkin, A.P. (1935) 'Anthropology in Australia, Past and Present' in *Australia and New Zealand Association for the Advancement of Science, Report* 22. pp. 196–207
—— (1939) 'Introduction' in Kaberry, P. *Aboriginal Woman: Sacred and Profane* London: Routledge
Gale, F. ed. (1974) *Women's Role in Aboriginal Society* 2nd edn, Canberra: Australian Institute of Aboriginal Studies
Gale, F. ed. (1983) *We are Bosses Ourselves: The Status and Role of Aboriginal Women Today* Canberra: Australian Institute of Aboriginal Studies
Gale, F. and Jacobs, J.M. (1987) *Tourists and the National Estate: Procedures to Protect Australia's Heritage* Canberra: Special Australian Heritage Publication No 6, Australian Heritage Commission
Goodale, J.C. (1971) *Tiwi Wives: A Study of the Women of Melville Island, Northern Australia* Seattle: University of Washington Press
Hamilton, A. (1975) 'Aboriginal Women: The means of production' in J. Mercer (ed.) *The Other Half: women in Australian society* Penguin Books, pp. 167–179
—— (1980) 'Dual Social System: Technology, Labour and Women's Secret Rites in the eastern Western Desert of Australia' *Oceania* 51, 1, pp. 4–19
—— (1981) 'A Complex Strategical Situation: Gender and Power in Aboriginal Australia' in N. Grieve and P. Grimshaw (eds) *Australian Women: Feminist Perspectives* Melbourne: Oxford University Press, pp. 69–85
Jacobs, J.M. (1983) 'Aboriginal Land Rights in Port Augusta', unpublished MA Thesis, University of Adelaide
—— (1985) 'Women Talking Up Big: Report on Aboriginal Women's Cultural Heritage Programme in Port Augusta' Adelaide: Aboriginal Heritage Branch, South Australian Department of Environment and Planning
—— (1988) 'The construction of identity' in J. Beckett (ed) *Aboriginal Identity and the Past* Canberra: Australian Institute of Aboriginal Studies pp 31–44

98 _Women, Rites and Sites_

—— (press) 'Politics and the cultural landscape: the case of Aboriginal land rights' _Australian Geographical Studies_

Jacobs, J.M., Laurence, C.O.M. and Thomas, F. (1988) ' "Pearls from the deep": re-evaluating the early history of Colebrook Home for Aboriginal children' in T. Swain and R.D. Bird (eds) _Aboriginal Australians and Christian Missions_ The Association for the Study of Religion

Kaberry, P. (1939) _Aboriginal Women: Sacred and Profane_ London: Routledge

Lamilami, L. (1974) _Lamilami Speaks: A Story of the People of Goulburn Islands, North Australia_ Sydney: Ure Smith

Maddock, K. (1974) _The Australian Aborigines: A Portrait of their Society_ London: Allen Lane

Reay, M. (1963) 'The social position of women' in H. Sheils (eds) _Australian Aboriginal Studies_ Melbourne: Oxford University Press, pp. 319–334

Shaw, B. and McDonald, S. (1978) 'They Did it Themselves: Reminiscences of Seventy Years' _Aboriginal History_ 2, 1, pp. 122–39

White, I. (1970) 'Aboriginal women's status: A paradox resolved' in F. Gale (ed.) _Women's Role in Aboriginal Society_ Canberra: Australian Institute of Aboriginal Studies, pp. 37–47

White, I., Barwick, D. and Meehan, B. (eds) (1985) _Fighters and Singers: the lives of some Australian Aboriginal women_ Sydney: Allen and Unwin

# 6

# THE STATUS OF WOMEN'S CULTURAL KNOWLEDGE
## Aboriginal society in north-east South Australia

### Luise Hercus

THE CLOSE links between the people of the Lake Eyre Basin were evident even to the earliest writers. We find for instance the following comment in Howitt and Siebert (1904: 101):

> They all belong to what may be called a nation, that is a group of tribes who are more or less akin to each other, whose languages are alike, or as to neighbouring tribes, merely dialects; who have the same class organisation under the names of Matterie and Kararu or their equivalents, and whose sacred ceremonies are practically the same.

This unity amid diversity is a most striking feature of the traditions of the Lake Eyre Basin. The languages and groupings of people in the area can be schematised as in Figure 6.1. People belonging to the same subgroup were closely connected and their languages were mutually comprehensible. Languages belonging to different subgroups, however, are not mutually comprehensible. All the people in the area, even those belonging to different language groups, were however linked by their joint traditions and their similar social structure.

In the mid 1960s Karangura and Wadikali had become extinct,

99

**Map 6.1 Tribal groupings in north-eastern South Australia based on Norman Tindale 1974**

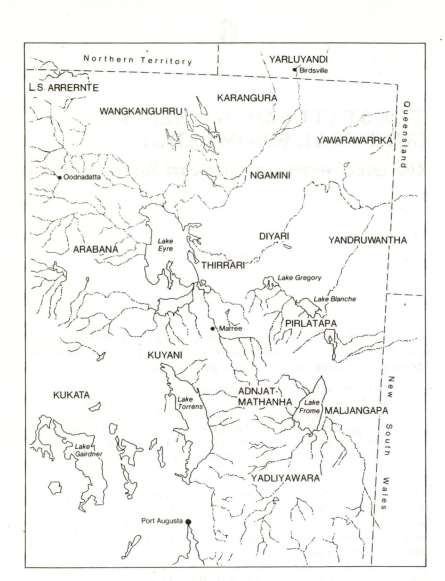

**Figure 6.1: Grouping of the Lake Eyre Basin languages**

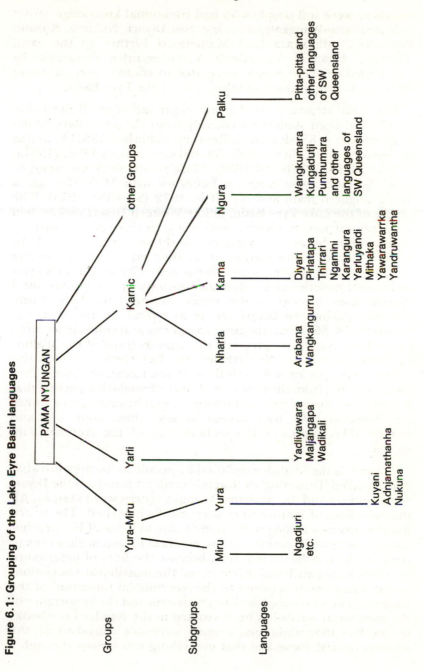

but there were still people who had traditional knowledge of not only Arabana–Wangkangurru, but also Diyari, Nukuna, Kuyani, Pirlatapa, Yadliyawara (and Maljangapa further to the east), Thirrari, Nagamini, Yarluyandi, Yandruwantha, Yawarawarrka and Mithaka. These people were able to confirm and elaborate what was known of the traditions of the Lake Eyre Basin.

The social structure and kinship organisation of all the Lakes people had been studied extensively from the early days of the large mission at Killalpaninna (Reuther, published 1981) as well as by Spencer and Gillen (1899: 58–68) onwards to Elkin (1931a, 1931b, 1938a, 1938b and 1939). More recent work was done by H.W. Scheffler, who came on fieldwork with Mick McLean (a Wangkangurru man) and myself in 1972 (Scheffler 1978). The people of the Lake Eyre Basin, unlike Western Desert people, had a matrilineal moiety system. According to this system a person inherits from his mother what he (or she) *is*, what he has as his essential 'flavour', his *mardu*, or as they say his 'meat' among Maljangapa and people further to the east. This division into two matrilineal moieties each subdivided into six or more matrilineal descent lines belongs to the whole of the Lake Eyre Basin. Scheffler (taking the Diyari system as typical for the area) has shown (1978: 363) that 'the basic categories and equivalence rules of the Dieri system are precisely the same as those of the Walbiri and Aranda systems'. Nevertheless the fact remains that in this system all people identify with their *mardu* totem, the totem they have inherited from their mother. It is the female descent line that is important. Senior men and senior women belonging to a *mardu* are *thidna-marduka* 'foot flavour bosses': they, both men and women alike, represent the embodiment of the Ancestors involved.

'History' is the English word used by people in the area for what is often called 'Dreaming' or 'totemic myth': it translates the Diyari word *pinthara* and the Arabana–Wangkangurru word *ularaka*. All the main lines of History were patrilineally inherited. The matrilineal *mardu* may belong to the same totem as a line of History, but does not necessarily entitle a *thidna-marduka* person of either sex to complete knowledge of that line, because the lines of inheritance for these were patrilineal. Elkin called the matrilineal associations 'social' totemism as opposed to the 'ceremonial totemism' of the *pinthara*. The whole approach to the system and the importance of the matrilineal *mardu* has been vitiated in the standard textbooks by the fact that traditional women were not consulted by the scholars quoted above and that everything was viewed through a sexual dichotomy. Writers have only recently begun to remedy this. Martin (1987: 8) has provided an excellent criticism of Elkin's view, stating: 'It seems that the division into matrilineal "social" and "ceremonial" totemism is more due to Elkin's functionalist anthropological paradigm than a reflection of what totemism was in these societies.'

From the evidence of the oldest speakers of Lake Eyre basin languages, recorded in the 1960s, the situation was as follows:

A man inherited his *marduka*, his association with the matrilineal *mardu*, from his mother; a woman would inherit it likewise, and they would indeed all have a secondary entitlement to the *ularaka* (*pinthara*) totemic line in question. A man would inherit his main *ularaka*, (*pinthara*) from his father and would learn the songs and ceremonies associated with it from his father and his father's side male relatives at the time of his initiation and subsequently. A woman would inherit likewise, but she would not, in traditional times, learn from her father, she would learn from her father's side female relatives. Depending on what the History was she would learn the whole or only parts of the song cycle involved, or a women's secret version. A third line of inheritance was through one's birth place. Everyone, male or female, would have a special relationship with their birth place and would learn the History connected with their birth place. Residence was always patrilocal and rights to 'country' came with the patrilineal *ularaka*. A person would also have a secondary right to her or his own mother's and paternal grandmother's birthplace.

To summarise, there were four forms of inheritance:
1. *Mardu*, 'flavour', is matrilineally inherited. It gives totemic identity but not a primary right to 'country'; *mardu* however gives a secondary right of access to the History connected with the *mardu* totem. This is passed on by a mother to her daughters and by the mother's brother to males.
2. History is primarily of patrilineal inheritance for both sexes: it gives right to country. A person may have several Histories.
3. Birth place, one's own place within the country of a local group. This gives right to History and hence to country.
4. This birth right is passed on by a woman to her son/ daughter, and then patrilineally to her grandson/ daughter.

The late Topsy McLean *Ikiwiljika* was typical of the women with traditional knowledge in the Lake Eyre Basin. She was born in 1898–9 near the Pudlowina *Pulawani* native well in the central Simpson Desert. She was full sister to Mick McLean, who described how she left the desert as a baby in 1900 (Hercus 1986). She was brought up by parents and relatives who had full traditional knowledge.

1. Her *mardu* (like her brother's) was *warrukathi*, Emu. Parts of the Emu History, *warrukathi ularaka*, were originally secret to men, so she was taught only the open sections of that History and she had secondary rights to country through that History. The country involved was the area surrounding *Papu-nginja* 'green egg' in the central Simpson desert, where the long Emu History started: this is where in the tradition the ancestral emus made their nest. The old man emu and the chicks walked about there, singing songs about the different plants they ate before starting on their long journey to the south-west. This section was non-secret. Subsequently Wangkangurru and Arabana men, at the instigation of one ritual leader, declared that the whole of this History should be open. Topsy McLean never did learn the entire cycle, though she had heard it.

2. Her father was ritual leader '*ularaka* boss' of the Two Men initiation cycle. She knew much of this myth but could not sing the songs. Her brother Mick however learnt these at his initiation. Her father's and brother's main *ularaka* was Rain. She knew the open sections of the Rain mythological cycle. Most importantly she too was a rain-maker in her own right and she was ritual leader of the women's Rain cycle, which she performed near Marree in January 1969. She had rights to land through the Rain cycle, but not to the main Rain centre at *Parra-parra* in the central Simpson Desert.

   She had her own main Rain-site, but owing to the factors outlined below, even she had only the haziest idea of where this site was, and there are reasons for thinking that it was in the vicinity of the lower southern Arrernte Rain ritual centre at Ilbora on the lower Finke.

3. Her birthplace near the *Pulawani* well was associated with grass seed increase, and she learnt the song cycle belonging to this. She had rights to *Pulawani* through this.

4. Her father's mother was born near *Urlita*, a great ritual centre for Grubs, Emu and Possum on the Finke in lower southern Arrernte country on the border of Wangkangurru country. Topsy could therefore call *Urlita* 'my country', and she had ceremonial rights there.

   There was thus traditionally a complex network of ownership of knowledge, *a network in which women had an important part.*

## Women's position in ritual

In the case of the Lake Eyre basin we are in the fortunate position of having access to reasonable information with regards to the traditional situation. The missionaries at Killalpaninna were paternalistic in the extreme, and they clearly expected Aboriginal society to be the same, but even they were aware of women taking part in ritual. Horne and Aiston (1924), basing their information mainly on traditional Wangkangurru people, were aware of the part played by women, they give an account of a large group of Cowarie people arriving at Mungeranie for a ceremony and women taking part (1924: 41–4). The best evidence of all comes from Wangkangurru people born in the Simpson Desert before direct white contact, who were still available in 1965 to give an account of how things had been. One thing is certain, the position of women in the ceremonial was quite different from that prevalent in the Western Desert. T.G.H. Strehlow (1970: 104) shows how there was a contrast between Arrernte and Western Desert as regards secrecy. He describes general Arrernte increase ceremonies and then states:

> The major 'Western Desert' type gatherings, on the other hand, were arranged for circumcision purposes—circumcision being visualised as the main act of initiating the male novice into the spiritual world of eternity. Hence all western desert verses that were sung on the circumcision grounds were regarded—unlike the corresponding Aranda verses—as being too sacred to be sung on any other occasion.

The contrast was even greater between Western Desert attitudes and attitudes among the Lakes people, as exemplified by Wangkangurru. Mick McLean Irinjili, raised in the Simpson Desert before direct white contact, was a strongly conservative and traditional-minded person. He was only too conscious of the concept of *thamunha* 'secret-sacred' *malka uljurlaru ngawinhanga* 'not to be heard by women'. He only passed on traditional knowledge to L. Hercus because she was an 'old woman', because there was no interested male research worker, because the tradition was in dire straits, and because the other senior Wangkangurru men, particularly his cousin George Kemp, constantly urged him to do this, and even then it was only after years of apprenticeship of learning the languages involved. Yet even he, Mick McLean, became irate whenever he heard of Western Desert ceremonies of the *Maliyara* 'Ring' type, when women were herded out of camp so that a secret ceremony could take place. He said on one of these occasions:

> I don't like this Maliyara they have. With us we *had* to have women there for every ceremony, we couldn't have it without them. Even 'putting boys through' women had to be there most of the time. The only one with no women was the Kangaroo, Antikirinja (*Western Desert*) people were in that too.

There was in fact one other exception apart from the Kangaroo History: rain-making ceremonies were usually conducted without women (see also Horne and Aiston 1924: 112). Women had their own secret rain-making ceremonies.

## Passing on knowledge

Open communal traditions, songs that were sung round the campfire at night, were gradually learnt by the young of both sexes from their earliest days. As for ritual traditions, since women had a part in nearly all ceremonies, much of the traditional oral literature and knowledge of sites was freely available. This however did not provide enough opportunity for learning: one does not learn at performances, one is supposed to learn at rehearsals.

In these days when traditional knowledge has declined so much one often hears talk of knowledge being 'handed over', or 'handed back'. Simple transference of knowledge is not possible: learning has been and probably always will be a long and painful process. It has been pointed out by Strehlow (1970: 104) that the corpus of oral traditions in Arrernte was vast, considerably more extensive than in the Western Desert and far beyond the capacity of any single person to master. The same applied to Arabana–Wangkangurru traditions and probably to those of other peoples of the Lake Eyre Basin. To learn even one of the *ularaka* traditions would have required months of repetition and study. Moreover, as shown very convincingly by Hale (1985), learning songs was not just repetition but also creativity, the intricacies and possibilities were so many that each creative person could leave an imprint on the traditions: they were ancient and yet living traditions. The study of these traditions required great effort and dedication, and unbelievable feats of memory. The social system, the 'gerontocracy' that one often associates with Aboriginal society ensured that the people with most leisure were those old men who were powerful enough to abrogate some of their practical responsibilities. Teen-age boys had plenty of time on account of their as yet limited responsibilities, so it was relatively easy to organise major instruction by the old men for boys before and after initiation. Increase in knowledge of traditions, both secret and non-secret would go on throughout a man's life.

Teenage girls learnt from their older female relatives, from their mothers and particularly from their father's sisters and father's mother. Because the society was patrilocal, the maternal grandmother was not normally present. They learnt to take part in ceremonies, both in women's secret ceremonies and in communal ceremonies. Instruction as in the case of men continued throughout life. Some matters were not handed on until a woman was considered an 'old woman', i.e. she was married and had children. The really old women often learnt songs and ceremonies and details of the mythology from their husbands and from other old men, particularly on occasions when old people could stay back in camp. Very frequently matters considered secret/sacred to men were passed on in this fashion, because the abhorrence against uttering anything secret was not so much against women as such, but against young uninitiated men. The fear that mothers would reveal secrets to their growing boys was not felt keenly in the case of these old women. Maudie Naylon *Akawiljika*, a Wangkangurru woman, (born Simpson Desert about 1886–7, dec. Birdsville 1981) gave an example of this. When she was in her late 40s on the Bluff Station near Birdsville she accidentally came across a cave containing sacred objects belonging to Mithaka men, who were notoriously severe in their discipline. They told her that if she had been a young woman they would have killed her, but she was 'old woman' and so they were not worried and even gave her information on the *ularaka*.

Maudie also confirmed the way in which traditions were passed on. On one of our visits with Mick McLean to her and her husband Bob at Birdsville, in 1972, Mick had, as usual, been spending day after day singing several lines of *ularaka*. He was about to start on another, when Maudie interrupted him. She was not being 'cheeky', she was the oldest person present and had an acknowledged right to speak as she did:

*Maudie.* I've been sitting here for a long time listening to you, so you keep quiet now and listen to me!
*Mick* and *Bob.* All right, but what are you going to sing?
*Maudie.* Just you keep quiet and listen!

Maudie then sang part of the Crane and Waterbird History.

*Maudie* continued: I know *all* that, all the way to *Pangalu*.
*Mick*. Whom did you get that from?
*Maudie*. That old woman gave me all this a long time ago.
*Mick*. Thara-nguyu ('One Thigh')?
*Maudie*. Don't! Don't name her!
*Mick*. She was my relation too.

The passing on of traditional knowledge is depicted diagrammatically in Figure 6.2.

Both men and women could attain to the exalted position of being 'clever', being a doctor *minparu*, Diyari *kunki*. This was known to Gason (1879: 283), and it was confirmed by the oldest Arabana and Wangkangurru people in the 1960s, but owing to the many changes militating against the status of women in the post-contact period there are no recent authenticated records of women doctors in the Lake Eyre Basin.

**Sites**

Because of their role in the ritual, women had access to practically all ceremonial and ancestral sites in Wangkangurru traditions. At certain times however, during the performance of secret sections of the ritual they were not permitted. The presence of women is confirmed by the archaeology of the Simpson Desert. Even at the

**Figure 6.2:** Lines of transmission of traditional knowledge in north-east South Australia

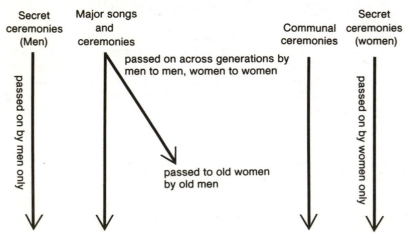

most sacred site of all, the initiation ritual centre at *MaRaru* (Hercus 1987) there were old grinding dishes, and men never used grinding dishes. Only the great Rain centre at *Parra-parra* showed no evidence of the presence of women (Clark, Hercus and Potezny, in preparation). Similarly in Arabana, Kuyani and Diyari country there were just a few locations where women were permanently excluded: these were mainly caves where sacred objects were housed (there are no caves in Wangkangurru country). Women were excluded, whether or not the objects were there at the time. Apart from these exceptional cases, exclusion of women was only temporary. Women were allowed to name all the sites and knew exactly where they were.

Men were, on a temporary basis, not permitted at sites where a secret women's ceremony was taking place, men were not even allowed to go out hunting in the same direction as groups of women going out for any reason, for ceremonies or ordinary food-gathering. In Wangkangurru traditions men had to go in the opposite direction and: 'not sneak round sideways; one fellow might be as bad as whitefellows are now, and anything might happen!'

The punishment was evil magic, that is the removal of his 'innards' and death within three days (Hercus MS.b). It seems that secrecy and exclusion of the opposite sex were not so much site-specific as activity specific.

As for 'country', everybody, male and female, knew their way round their own country in incredible detail. The late Dora Parker (Yarluyandi) has given dramatic accounts of people travelling through the Georgina country at night, because it was impossible to travel in the heat of day. The question of getting lost simply never occurred, and Dora described how her old grandmother could even in total darkness tell the difference between various types of snakes. If one had to make an invidious comparison between male and female knowledge of 'country' in traditional times, the available evidence suggests that men's knowledge was probably more far-flung, and women's knowledge more detailed.

## Changes in the post-contact period

The system of transmission outlined above meant that there was constant change and constant development in the cultural knowledge of women, depending on the efficiency of the various lines of transmission. The European presence changed all this. The main factors involved were the following:

1. increased secrecy;
2. revivalist movements—a positive change;
3. separation from 'country';
4. European attitudes;
5. ignorance.

*Increased secrecy*

In the latter half of the 19th century traditional owners in the Lake Eyre basin gradually felt more and more threatened. This was through the general disruption of the traditional way of life. The old men felt that their authority was waning and they became increasingly suspicious of the younger generation. They feared that young men were not paying enough respect to traditions, wanting to get hold of information too quickly and easily and not 'the hard way' as they themselves had done. From then on they became more and more 'cunning', i.e. devious in withholding information from others. This naturally affected all the lines of transfer of information including those to and among women. The trend was not universal: there were some old people who were worried about the loss of traditions and therefore took the opposite line and made things more open, as in the case of the Emu History, but on the whole there was a general disruption of transfer of knowledge. This situation has been described clearly by T.G.H. Strehlow (1970: 115).

The part played by Spencer and Gillen in this increased secrecy is described by Strehlow for southern Arrernte people. It had an even more direct impact in Arabana country, combined with the 'invasion' by Antikirinja people belonging to the Western Desert. Spencer and Gillen worked with Arabana men at the Peake in 1901 and 1912 (Mulvaney and Calaby 1984). They concentrated on obtaining detailed anthropological and ritual information from the senior men. These enquiries were unprecedented in their scope and led to recriminations for many years to come: there are recorded accounts of this (Hercus MSa). Some old men are said to have been 'boned' by others for allegedly divulging matters that did not 'belong' to them. Others were blamed for the increasing inroads of Antikirinja people because they had sung their own country to strangers, and again there were killings, not only of Arabana men by Antikirinja men, but of Arabana amongst themselves. The late Mick McLean considered this to have been a major factor in the dramatic decline in Arabana population during the period of World War I. In this atmosphere of hatred and distrust there was a real breakdown of the old established lines of transmission, and this naturally had an adverse effect on the continuation of knowledge, particularly as far as women were concerned.

### Revivalist movements—a positive change

There were two great ceremonies in the eastern Lake Eyre Basin which involved practically the whole population of the area in a series of rituals in which everybody took part: it was inconceivable to have them without women. One was the *Mindiri*, which was basically an emu increase ritual and which belonged to all the people of the Cooper and adjoining areas. The three most important ritual centres for this were the Wadrawadrinna water-hole near Innamincka, Cooncherie waterhole north-east of Clifton Hills, and Lake Howitt. The *Mindiri* could be performed at other sites too, there are records of it being performed at Koppera-manna, and on the shores of the huge claypan called Lake Etamunbanie, east of Pandie Pandie. The second great ceremony was the *Warrthampa* which belonged to the people living further north, the Yarluyandi, Wangkangurru, Mithaka and their neighbours. Both ceremonies had always provided joyous occasions for the whole population and were important for social and material exchange. By the latter part of last century however, these large gatherings provided an opportunity for massacres, which practically wiped out several groups of people (Hercus 1986). Both ceremonies involved what is usually described as 'sexual licence', and were therefore particularly abhorrent to the missionaries. Performances continued, but on a much reduced scale.

During the same period, the latter part of last century, there evolved a new type of great ceremony, which, unlike the *Mindiri* and the *Warrthampa* was not connected with 'country' nor with increase, nor with any particular ancestor. These 'travelling' ceremonies embodied a revival of the joy of composition, dancing and music-making and they were at least to some extent a form of self-assertion and a protest against European oppression. They were all entirely non-secret and both men and women took part. Three great ceremonies had an impact in South Australia, particularly for the self-esteem of women. They were:
  i. the *Mudlungga;*
  ii. the *Wantji-wantji;*
  iii. the *Unintha;*
and there was a fourth which was more localised,
  iv. the *Karlapa.*
  The *Mudlungga* is the best known of the travelling ceremonies. It

has been discussed by writers from Roth (1897) and Gregory (1906) onwards. It came from the north and became known to people along the Diamantina in far western Queensland, and they in turn handed it down further south. Mick McLean gave a detailed description of how he and other young Wangkangurru people, male and female, all danced this corroboree in 1901, showing it and teaching it to one group after another. Even now, in 1988, there are still two people, husband and wife, who have knowledge of some verses from the *Mudlungga*.

The *Wantji-wantji* was said to be a wild and rough corroboree for men: 'you get a hiding in that!' Women joined in both the singing and the dancing. In the version seen by Daisy Bates (1966: 125) there was a section from which women were excluded. The *Wantji-wantji* came from the west and was introduced to Arabana and Kuyani people at Finniss springs. A Kukata man, 'Cranky' Alec from Roxby and his wife Alice, the last Kuyani, were leaders of the ceremony, which became known as 'the Roxby corroboree'. Alice played a major part in the whole organisation. There are accounts of the ceremony from several women who witnessed it at Finniss in about 1930. They recalled how a young boy, who had never before seen a ceremony, thought it might be fun to use a torch to embarrass the naked male dancers. It was Alice who put a stop to this at once and there was no further trouble. There is still one older Arabana woman who can sing some verses of the *Wantji-wantji*.

The *Unintha* was a women's dance. Spencer and Gillen saw it at Charlotte Waters in 1901 and described it as 'monotonous' (Mulvaney 1982: 40) though they appreciated the decorations of the dancers. Spencer took an excellent photograph. The corroboree was brought into South Australia and was apparently performed at Curdimurka early this century. Traditional ceremonies were no longer being regularly performed and the *Unintha* became a great favourite—in the end it was because the women wore beautiful painted decorations but no clothes while dancing. In the 1960s, long after this ceremony had ceased to be performed, the eyes of even the most respectable old men still invariably lit up at the mere mention of the *Unintha*, and it seems that it had ultimately become the equivalent of a nightclub act. Nobody in South Australia can·sing it now.

There must have been more to the *Unintha* than the dancing or perhaps it became more elaborate as it spread through South Australia towards the east. Cecil 'Knocker' Ebsworth, a Wangku-mara man from Nockatunga in Queensland, described a ceremony called *Ngunintha* which he had seen at Tibooburra as a child in the 1920s. (As Wangkumara does not have initial vowels, *Ngunintha* corresponds exactly to *Unintha*). He remembers it to this day as a great occasion with women and men dancing, one acting out the part of a 'devil-devil' and with other solos and groups. A much older Wangkumara speaker, Jack O'Lantern, remembered verses from it.

The *Karlapa* is a relatively late creation: it is said to have been composed early this century by an old man at Anna Creek for the benefit of Arabana women. Old Alice also had a hand in the composition. The *Karlapa* was known as 'the Anna Creek corroboree', and the name presumably comes from *Karla Tjarlpa*, the Arabana word for Anna Creek. The *Karlapa* was an elaborate spectacle with women dancing in groups, duets and solos, elaborately painted. The story revolved round two young women and a man in a drought and carrying waterbags. It was initially a performance that could be seen by everybody, and sections of it included male dancers. It was performed wherever there were groups of Arabana people. Diyari women began to learn it too. By the time I saw it near Marree in 1969—with old Alice singing—the matter of paint in lieu of clothes had become so embarrassing that it was definitely for women only. What had been created as a ceremony for general entertainment had become segregated.

*Separation from 'country'*

As was pointed out long ago by Horne and Aiston (1924: 10), one of the first effects of white occupation was the abandonment of the prohibitions regarding entry into other people's country. There was large scale migration in the Lake Eyre Basin. Wangkangurru people left their country altogether, and people from throughout the area congregated at Killalpaninna, and to a lesser extent at Marree and at Andrewilla in Yarluyandi country south of Birdsville. This meant that people became dissociated from their own 'country' and hence from their History. This applied much more to women than to men. Previously men, women and children had travelled as local groups within their own country and to ritual centres. Only on rare occasions men went on their own far afield on ochre expeditions. Now the boundaries no longer operated, and furthermore there were rations for the families. The older men, not working, were now on a permanent holiday. They were free to leave their families at ration centres if they felt inclined to visit their own country or travel generally. The oldest man from the Lake Eyre Basin, Ben Murray, speaking in Wangkangurru and English, gave a graphic account of this happening among Wangkangurru people living at the turn of the century at Muloorina. He recounted the peregrinations of one old man, Punjili. (Austin, Hercus and Jones forthcoming).

## PUNJILI

1. *muyu    nguru    thangka-rda    kanhangarda,    thika-rnda*
   Day     other    stay-PRES      there,          return-PRES

   *Marri-riku-lki,    Marri-riku-lki    thika-rnda,    Mundowdna*
   Marree-ALL-FIN,    Marree-ALL-FIN    return-PRES,   Mundowdna

   *thika-rnda,*    might be *muyu nguy,*    might be *muyu parkulu.*
   return-PRES      day one,                day two.

2. *tharpa-tharpa-rnda,    tharpa-arpa-rnda    Punjili    pidla.*
   trample on-PRES,        trample down-PRES   Punjili    name.

3. In English

4. *'antha    yuka-rnda-lki    thidnangkara,    thidnangkara    antha*
   'I         go-PRES-FIN      north,           north           I

   *yuka-rnda    mayi!    nhanhi    ngarrkani    idnhi-rnda!'*
   go-PRES,      hey!     look      moon         is-PRES!'

   that moon there, it must be just about half way between new and quarter!.

5. In English
   (Grammatical abbreviations used: PRES — present tense, ALL — allative FIN — a particle indicating finality)

## TRANSLATION

1. He (Punjili, an old Wangkangurru man) would stay there (at Muloorina) for a couple of days, and then go back to Marree. He would go to Marree, to Mundowdna and then he would be back again, maybe for one day, maybe for two.
2. 'Trampling underfoot' that is the meaning of the name Punjili.
3. He could go to the Kallakoopah and then go on to the desert. He used to travel around that way, and leave his wife. He would say:
4. 'I am going away now to the north, it is to the north that I am going. Hey, just look at the moon! That moon there, it must be just about half way between new and quarter!'
5. Well that is the time he'd be back. He'd work it right too! Grandfather went too. Only my grandmother and the other women stayed on living there, and maybe another man who was too old, and he was blind too. He was Diyari.

This meant that men were free to live out and refresh their traditions, and even increase their knowledge. Women, however, could only go on performing their own ceremonies in isolation: women were further and further removed from their country and the source of their traditions.

As for the younger people, it often happened that Aboriginal women as well as men were employed working with stock and they travelled around the station—which was of course not always part of their own country. At least this meant that both men and women alike saw 'country'. Thus Topsy McLean Ikiwiljika got to know much of Peake station because she was working there, helping with the mustering. With the increasing prevalence of the European paternalistic approach, both at the mission and at the stations, women were gradually relegated to cleaning and cooking jobs around the homesteads, and most of them had little opportunity of seeing any 'country', their own or anybody else's.

## European attitudes

For a variety of reasons, none of the early investigators in the Lake Eyre Basin asked women about traditional knowledge; women tended to be ignored. This had repercussions: the things that the great scholars of the past were interested in—particularly initiation ritual—obviously gained in prestige, the things they never asked about were suspected of not being worth knowing. This situation continued into the present century. Thus during the 1934 Museum expedition to the Diamantina, leading men made recordings of short passages of traditional song. Many senior women were present, including the ritual owner of the Yarluyandi Swan History. In the film of the expedition (made available to Aboriginal people in Birdsville by P. Jones) women are featured only as showing their 'domestic' skills, winnowing and grinding seed and digging up wild onions.

These attitudes must have contributed to a general loss of status. The worst blow for the status of women's cultural knowledge in the Lake Eyre Basin was the arrival from about 1900 onwards of large numbers of people of Western Desert origin, particularly Antikirinja on Anna Creek station, at Oodnadatta and Macumba, and of Kukata people on Stuart Creek station. Amongst these Western Desert people women had separate knowledge and separate sites, but the overall responsibility was male. Arabana women had not previously had the same need for separate sites, and so they found themselves altogether disinherited. This led to a clear-cut distinction between the situation that prevails in Birdsville and originally prevailed in Marree, as opposed to Oodnadatta. In Oodnadatta men's and women's traditions are segregated. In Marree, people used to defer to Old Alice, because she was the oldest and most knowledgeable person as well as being a Kuyani in Kuyani country. In Birdsville likewise responsibility went strictly with age and knowledge, and it still does so. When in the early 1970s a landowner cut down more and more of the rare wadi trees (*Acacia peuce*) at the one main site where they grow near Birdsville, it was not the old men, but Maudie Naylon *Akawiljika* who told him not to destroy the trees belonging to the History. He stopped.

*Ignorance*

Because of the breakdown of transference of information, younger people simply ceased to have an opportunity to learn about traditions in the Lake Eyre Basin, but those at Oodnadatta and more recently even those living at Marree saw traditions alive and well amongst their western neighbours. Many began to believe that an important site was a secret/sacred site and an initiation site, and not necessarily one that was celebrated in song and ritual and known to all. 'Important' became equivalent *not* to 'significant in myth and song', *but* to 'no women allowed'. Women were therefore absent from the 1983 debate about the site at Cane Grass Swamp *Piya-piyanha*. This belonged to the History of the two snakes *Kurkari* and *Yurkunangku*, a History that was once open to all, and which was known to the oldest women. Mount O'Halloran North near Oodnadatta is 'the woman's head' which the ancestor *Wilkurda* cut off: her trunk is said to be the flat platform that is Toondina Spring. Because it was suddenly assumed that the site was secret/sacred, women and children were at one stage forbidden to have their usual picnics there. Later it was thought that the *Wampitji* 'rainbow' cave on the way to Macumba was something to do with *wanpatjara* 'nightowl' and therefore 'dangerous'. It was simply because the people concerned did not know the meaning of the word *wampitji* that there was a thought of excluding women. Incidents of this kind are very frequent in the eastern states, where the loss of traditions has gone much further. Ignorance nevertheless has been playing an increasing role in the exclusion of women from sites even in South Australia. Ignorance has brought about the view that women were always excluded and therefore had no knowledge of traditions.

**The present**

Because in the Lake Eyre Basin secrecy was mainly activity-specific rather than site-specific, special women's secret sites were probably not nearly as numerous or significant as in the Western Desert.

The lower Southern Arrernte situation was somewhere in between those two extremes and by the early 1960s the oldest surviving lower southern Arrernte women had some knowledge of sites in the Dalhousie area. They referred to a woman's rain site which was a rock with a waterfall in the desert, probably a reference to one of the outermost channels of the Finke.

There are numerous mythical and actual dancing grounds for women. The *Urumbula* native cat cycle describes the journey of Malbunga, the cat ancestor from Port Augusta to Alice Springs. At most of the main places where the cat people are said to have camped there are mythical women's dancing grounds, usually claypans rather smaller than the adjoining mythical men's dancing grounds. The best known of these were near Yellow Waterhole (the road now goes right through this dancing ground) and near Bottom Waterhole on Brown's Creek. Similarly the *Mindiri* involves special women's dancing grounds, such as a smaller claypan near the main men's ground, Lake Howitt. These are not secret women's grounds.

## Women's knowledge of sites

Throughout the Lake Eyre Basin, as a result of European influence, women suffered greatly from their lack of mobility and therefore had less chance to keep in touch with sites than did men. There are however notable exceptions: Old Alice (Kuyani) had grown up before the worst of the lack of mobility hit women, and she knew Kuyani country very well. Her blindness was even more of a tragedy on account of this. Today, despite all odds, there are still women with a knowledge of sites. The senior Wangkangurru person at Birdsville spent most of her life in Yarluyandi country south of Birdsville, which traditionally belonged to her mother and to her grandmother Judy Trew *Tandripilinha*. She can still sing the Swan History, and she learnt from them about sites all along the Diamantina and down as far as Mount Gason. She knows the names and stories of all the waterholes around Goyder's Lagoon, she can even name the more prominent sandhills. She knows the country further east too, around *Ngapa-mana* Minnie Downs. Neither her husband nor her elder brother had quite the same thorough acquaintance with Yarluyandi country. Both these men knew a wider area, because they had travelled further and learnt from the old men, and they could each sing a different History, but knowledge of the details of Yarluyandi country is exclusively hers.

A senior woman originally from Macumba has knowledge not only of the Macumba area and the associated Fire History, but also of the Memory Bore–Three Forges area. Several other women have knowledge of specific sites, one knows about Kirrawadinna Creek near Mungeranie on the Birdsville Track, another has some knowledge of Murnpeowie country. In their youth these senior women were all involved in kitchen and ironing duties on stations, but they were determined to get away for long enough to learn something about the country. They succeeded.

*Language*

This is a field in which women are outstanding. The most fluent speaker of Wangkangurru and the only person who knows some Yarluyandi is a woman. The only three speakers of Diyari are women, and two of the three best speakers of Arabana are women.

Some of the factors that militated against women as regards their knowledge of 'country' have favoured their ability to retain the language: they have moved about less and have been exposed to fewer extraneous influences. Invariably it was the women who stayed home and spent years of their lives caring for their aged grandparents and parents, and they therefore were inevitably exposed to the traditional languages. Even if, under the stresses and strains of ordinary life, they may have found it tiresome to 'listen to grandma', they could not help but learn, with the result that today they are the mainstay of the traditional languages.

*Other traditional and historical knowledge*

As women were traditionally the gatherers of vegetable foods, they have retained a better knowledge of edible plants and also of herbal remedies. Most of the senior women in the Lake Eyre Basin are knowledgeable in this field. They remember all kinds of cultural matters ranging from how to identify a murderer to how to make *malthirri*, the special cakes made for men taking part in initiation ceremonies. They can recall trips to the Mulligan to collect pitcheri, they remember the Basedow expedition, the setting up of the mission at Finniss and all kinds of historical data.

All the senior women have an unrivalled knowledge of who is who in the Lake Eyre Basin, they can recall genealogies, tribal affiliations and stories about people. They excel in all matters of human interest. Unfortunately most of the younger generation are not listening to them now.

**References**

Austin, P., Hercus, L.A. and Jones, P. (forthcoming) 'Ben Murray'
  *Aboriginal History*

Bates, D. (1966) 2nd ed. *The Passing of the Aborigines* Melbourne: Heinemann; London: John Murray

Buckley, R., Ellis, C.J., Hercus, L., and White, I.M. (1968) *'Group Project on Andagarinja Women'* Vol 2, Adelaide: private publication, University of Adelaide Library

Clark, P., Hercus, L.A. and Potezny, V. (in preparation), 'The Rain-site at Parra-para'

Elkin, A.P. (1931) 'The Social Organisation of South Australian Tribes' *Oceania* 2, pp. 44–73

—— (1938–40) 'Kinship in South Australia' *Oceania* 8, pp. 419–452; 19, 41–78; 10, pp. 295–399

Gason, S. (1879) 'The manners and customs of the Dieyerie Tribe of Australian Aborigines' in J.D. Woods *Native Tribes of South Australia* Adelaide: Cox

Gregory, J.W. (1906) *The dead Heart of Australia* London: John Murray

Hercus, L.A. (MSa) Mr Spencer

—— (MSb) Killing by Magic

—— (1980) ' "How we danced the Mudlungga": Memories of 1901 and 1902' *Aboriginal History* 4, pp. 5–31

—— (1986) 'The end of the Mindiri people' in L.A. Hercus and P. Sutton *This is what happened* Canberra: Australian Institute of Aboriginal Studies

—— (1986a) 'Leaving the Simpson Desert' *Aboriginal History* 9, pp. 22–43

Horne, G.A. and Aiston, G (1924) *Savage Life in Central Australia* London: Macmillan

Howitt, A.W. and Siebert, O. (1904) 'Legends of the Dieri and kindred tribes of Central Australia' *Journal of the Royal Anthropological Institute* 34, pp. 100–129

Martin, D. (1987) 'An Anthropological Survey for Sites of Significance to the Olympic Dam Township, Marree' Canberra: Anutech

Mulvaney, D.J. (1982) *The Aboriginal Photographs of Baldwin Spencer* Melbourne: John Currey, O'Neill, National Museum of Victoria

Mulvaney, D.J. and Calaby, J.H. (1984) *'So much that is new' Baldwin Spencer 1860–1929* Melbourne: Melbourne University Press

Reuther, G.J. (1981) *The Diari*, Vols 1–13, translated by P. Scherer, AIAS microfiche No. 2 Canberra: Australian Institute of Aboriginal Studies

Roth, E. (1897) *Ethnological studies among the north-west central Queensland Aborigines* Brisbane: Government Printer

Spencer, B. and Gillen, F. (1899) *The Native Tribes of Central Australia* London: Macmillan

Strehlow, T.H.G. (1970) 'Geography and the Totemic Landscape in Central Australia: a functional study' in R.M. Berndt (ed) *Australian Aboriginal Anthropology* Nedlands WA: University of WA Press, pp. 92–140

# 7

## ROLES REVISITED
### The women of southern South Australia

### Fay Gale

WHY IS it that today it is so often Aboriginal women who convey an impression of strength and resoluteness, yet history portrays them as weak and completely dominated by Aboriginal men? Have the women changed dramatically since white settlement or has non-Aboriginal society been grossly misled in its view of the position of women in Aboriginal society?

The most detailed descriptions of the status of Aboriginal women at Point McLeay are those given by the first missionary to that station, George Taplin. In his diary for September 22, 1859, he wrote, 'The women are real slaves and are bartered continually, and so much below the brute are they that . . . few husbands expect constancy in their wives, but many actually encourage and command the reverse'.

When I first came to know women from Point McLeay I was impressed by their strength of character and independence of mind. It was only later that I read Taplin and other 19th century recorders and found it impossible to reconcile the two very different views. Was it that I was a woman talking to women, while most recorders last century were men, or had Aboriginal women changed since Europeans arrived?

As has already been indicated elsewhere in this volume, early opinions of the status of Aboriginal women in their society were strongly influenced by popular views of the time.

The Darwinian theory of a 'scale of evolution' and the 'survival of the fittest' permitted even the most liberal of colonisers to justify the European settlement and usurpation of Aboriginal lands, and even the genocide of the original occupants, in the name of science. It is perhaps not surprising that a belief in the evolutionary superiority of Europeans also lead to an assumption that Aboriginal women were scarcely human.

At the time when such views were prevalent, southern South Australia was studied by a number of observers, trained scientists and explorers. The more particular of the observers recorded descriptions and activities of Aboriginal women not always in accord with popular opinion of the day. Whilst the views of observers such as Sturt and Eyre were undoubtedly clouded by their culture and its ethnocentrism, nevertheless they described events and situations that give a reasonably positive view of the status of women in southern South Australia at the time of European settlement.

The earliest visitor to southern South Australia who kept relatively detailed and seemingly accurate journals was Charles Sturt. He followed the River Murray to its mouth during 1829–30, some six years prior to the official settlement of South Australia. Although Sturt's descriptions of the Aboriginal people suggest they may already have had contact with Europeans or at least their diseases, no earlier written record of the lower Murray survives.

Probably the most important early recorder was Edward John Eyre. Eyre, like Sturt, was an explorer, but in 1844 he accepted a government position as sub-protector of Aborigines and resident magistrate at Moorundie, a settlement established on the River Murray. The government station was set up as a ration depot to attract Aborigines and keep them there by means of regular rations of food. The idea was to pacify them and thus ensure a safer passage for the drovers or overlanders who were bringing sheep from New South Wales to settle in South Australia.

Eyre was a careful observer whose sympathy for Aboriginal people is at odds with the attitude of most of his peers. Both because of the length of time he spent in the area and because of his apparent attention to detail in writing his diaries, the records of this man are quite important in reaching an understanding of the Aboriginal people of the area early in the contact period.

As a European, born and bred in Britain, we would expect Eurocentric views to dominate his perception. As a 19th century male, we would expect his views on women, especially those of 'native' women, to be rather chauvinistic. Furthermore, we assume that as a man he would have had only limited access to situations that might have informed him about the social and religious status of Aboriginal women in their own culture. Not surprisingly, males predominate in his views and his description of the Murray people as they were only a decade after the colonisation of South Australia.

In spite of the limitations, we do learn quite a substantial amount from Eyre about the status of women and, given all the biases through which the information has been filtered, the end product is surprisingly positive. One gleans from his diaries a view of Aboriginal women as much more independent and socially important than our 20th century views have usually led us to believe.

It has been especially in the religious and cultural sphere that women have usually been described as uninvolved, unimportant, indeed often even lacking religious or ceremonial knowledge at all. Yet in Eyre's meticulous reports are to be found frequent descriptions of women's ceremonial knowledge and involvement in religious activities.

When describing the ceremonial life of the southern Murray people, with whom he lived, he discusses dances in which men and women jointly participated and he decribes ceremonies for men only; but he also refers to ceremonies for women only. It is quite clear that Eyre realised there were three kinds of ceremonies: joint occasions, all male activities and (unlike most other scholars) he also knew that there were ceremonies for women only. One description of a joint ceremony reads thus (Eyre, 1845: 231)

> The females of the tribe exhibiting, generally sit down in front of the performers, either irregularly, in a line, or a semi-circle, folding up their skin cloaks into a hard ball and then beating them upon their laps with the palms of their hand, and accompanying the noise thus produced with their voices. . .

He also shows quite clearly that apart from combined ceremonies there were separate women's rituals (Eyre,1845: 228):

> In some of the dances only are women allowed to take part; but they have dances of their own, in which the men do not join . . .

Was Eyre a more careful observer than even the professional ethnographers, who came later? Did Eyre come closer to a full understanding of the various aspects of Aboriginal life because he lived with the one group for several years? Was it just that he wrote what he knew without being hampered by the cultural blinkers of later students of Aboriginal society? It is evident that he went into a completely unknown situation and recorded it.

Eyre was apparently open minded enough to distinguish between joint ceremonies where men took the leading part and those where women were the chief participants.

> In a dance which women are the chief performers, their bodies are painted with white streaks, and their hair adorned with cockatoo feathers. They carry large sticks in their hands, and place themselves in a row in front, whilst the men with their spears stand in a line behind them. They then all commence their movements, but without intermingling, the males and females dancing by themselves. (Eyre, 1845: 235)

All such activities could be observed by males and females. Eyre does not describe any activities which could be categorised purely as women's business, except to make it clear that he knew such existed. There would therefore seem to be little excuse for later observers to say that being male they did not have access to women's business and thus did not know about it. They usually did not even bother to record female participation in the joint ceremonies.

Eyre's careful use of language suggests his sensitivity to the activities of women, as well as those of the males which he knew more about. For example, when he discusses women's tattoos, something which could scarcely be hidden after the event, he describes their making as the only female 'ceremony of importance that I am aware of' (Eyre, 1845: 340). These tattoos were performed on the backs of young women and during the ceremony the mother of the girl being operated upon would 'lament' and mourn, accompanied by several other adult women (Eyre, 1845: 342). Following the ceremony, the girl appeared smeared with grease and ochre and wearing two kangaroo teeth and a tuft of emu feathers in her hair.

Eyre does not draw conclusions from his observations, and fortunately so since the bald facts carry more credibility than commentary would have done. Nevertheless, the evidence is fairly plain. This ceremony, with all of its preparation and elaborate associations, must have been a female equivalent of the initiation at puberty of young men. Eyre states that girls were anxious to have the ceremony performed and took great pride in the scarred evidence of their womanhood.

Eyre describes, but in less detail, the tattooing ceremonies of older women, when arms or abdomen would also be scarred. He also refers to other female ceremonies that presumably he heard about, rather than actually witnessed. The tattooing would have been quite evident and indeed was proudly paraded after the event. This was not the case with some other, apparently more private, women's activities. He does mention the fact that a woman's pubic hair was plucked after the death of a child and 'sometimes from other causes' (Eyre, 1845: 343) but he does not elaborate further.

With such records, even those lacking the detail that a female observer may have been able to add, it is impossible to deny the existence of ceremonies that were solely for women, or the participation of women in the wider religious life of the community.

Why then did other contemporary observers see or acknowledge so little of the role or significance of women? From Sturt we can expect nothing more than the factual recordings of when and where he saw people and what they looked like, since he traversed the Murray to explore it and not its people. He did not stay with any one group for a period of time as Eyre did.

Other observers with more opportunity to obtain further details than Sturt could have done also give us little insight into the position of women or of their religious or ceremonial function. Undoubtedly the fact that all the early observers were men would have prevented them from exploring much of the secret life of women, but, as Eyre has demonstrated, there is much that men could have observed had they cared to do so. We can thus only assume that the early British inhabitants of southern areas of South Australia had cultural blinkers that prevented them from seeing what was in front of their very eyes. It is undoubtedly this cultural blindness that has remained until the present day rather than the mere fact of the maleness of the observers.

Stephens (1839) for instance, recorded the attendance of women at ceremonies and described their musical accompaniment but saw them as very much a secondary force. He reported a dance similar to that described by Eyre but did so in different tones. His observations were of the people on the Adelaide plains and in the Encounter Bay region but his inaccurate generalisations are evident in the first sentence of the following quotation. His view of women's role in ceremonies should be viewed with similar questioning: (Stephens, 1839: 8):

> The corroboree is danced exactly as in other parts of New
> Holland. The women and children sit upon the ground
> around a fire, and before each of them a bundle is placed
> over which is bound tightly a piece of kangaroo skin; this they
> strike with their fists in remarkably exact time, singing

simultaneously in a monotonous but not distinct style. The men and boys are the only dancers . . .

There are no further references to women's ceremonies.

Cawthorne (1844), also describing the Kaurna of the Adelaide plains, says: 'The diversions of the women consist merely in participation in those of the men' (Cawthorne, 1844: 60). As illustration he says that the women tend to sing and beat sticks in corroborees while the men dance. Wallace, a resident of Millicent in the south-east of the State, in 1859 recorded gatherings of Aboriginal people at Mt. Burr. 'The women did the singing and beat their sticks on rolled-up opossum skin rugs' (Campbell, 1934: 31).

Such observers saw the involvement of women in ceremonies as secondary to that of the men and did not appear to notice or hear of other ceremonial activities such as those recorded by Eyre. But they did acknowledge the participation of women in the major ceremonies—later ethnographers give the impression that all of the major events were for males only.

Unfortunately none of the earliest writers were women, however even when women did begin to write about Aboriginal people in southern South Australia they did not seem to see any more than did their white male counterparts. In fact, most fieldworkers in the second part of the 19th century in the southern part of the State were missionaries or 'philanthropists'. Their concern was more with 'rescuing' Aboriginal women than with recording their 'pagan' beliefs. Mrs James Smith (1880) has several descriptions of female conversions from a life of 'drunkenness' and 'rudeness' and reports of conversions to Christianity but, although being a woman herself, she does not discuss Aboriginal women from a cultural or traditional view point except in the retailing of myths. She does however give some insight into areas not recorded by the male ethnographers of the time. For example, she discusses child birth and the role of midwives. But she also makes strong culturally biased statements in a very generalised fashion. For example: 'Many of the women ate their offspring: they said it was part of their flesh and made them strong' (Smith, 1880: 8).

Mrs Smith (whose first name does not appear in the book) records the ill-treatment of women and gives sound rationalisation for intervention by missionaries. 'It is the usual custom for a woman, after her husband dies, to be forced to lead an immoral life, under the care (!) of the nearest relative' (Smith, 1880: 13).

In this, Mrs Smith resembles male recorders last century in this area. 'Wives are regarded as absolute property and are exchanged or bartered away at the whim of the husband' (Cawthorne, 1844: 75).

George Taplin, who was a missionary to the southern people from 1859 to 1879, kept extensive records in a daily diary. He also published much of the material when he retired. He describes the women thus: 'Their licentiousness is dreadful. The demon sin seems to have trampled female virtue and connubial love out of their bosoms' (Diaries, 22 September 1859: 220). Such interpretations were, of course, intrinsic to missionary activity at that time. But Taplin lived with the people he had gathered at Point McLeay mission from the southern areas of the lower Murray, Adelaide and the lakes for 20 years. He came to know them well over this considerable period of time and obviously became very attached to them as people as well as potential converts. His records are thus quite contradictory, speaking at one time as a missionary and an Englishman, but at another as a relatively objective observer less blinkered by his own cultural biases.

On the one hand he can say that women do not feel grief at the death of a husband although they put on a great show of mourning. His rationale is the assumption that the women are so badly treated by men they are not sorry to see them die. 'The lamentations of the women are only conventional, except a few individuals. It is hard to see why a slave should wail for her tyrant, who has oppressed her all his life, and whose property she became by force' (Diaries, 14 November 1859).

On the other hand, Taplin makes simple statements of observation without western interpretation such as: 'It is a practice among the Aborigines never to get wives from their own tribe' (Diaries, 28 May 1859). Or, as evidence of his ability to be objective: 'Aboriginal women generally suffer less on the whole during parturition than white women do. I attribute this to their bodies being allowed to develop in childhood without the restraints and injuries which result from the use of stays, corsets and other civilised appliances' (Taplin, 1877:48).

However, we learn little about the religious and ceremonial roles of Aboriginal women. Taplin leaves us with the same impression that most ethnographers until very recently have given, namely that women were largely irrelevant in the whole religious/spiritual sphere. Indeed as one seeking to convert the people away from their own religious beliefs and practices, he saw the women whom he assumed had less religious involvement as easier targets than the men. 'It is much pleasanter to deal with the women than the men. They are so much more tractable' (Diaries, 27 January 1860). 'The women listened to me with much attention, especially when I told them of the resurrection and last judgement' (Diaries, 25 June 1859). He considered his first convert to be a woman called Teenminne (Diaries, 8 December 1859).

Later missionaries and recorders were even more convinced that it was the men who possessed the religious knowledge and control. But for Eyre, we might still be as blinded as were our forebears concerning the ceremonial roles of Aboriginal women in southern South Australia.

We learn more about women's ceremonies from Eyre, than we do from women observers such as Mrs James Smith or Janet Matthews, the missionary at Manunka on the River Murray. Mrs. Matthews wrote a great deal about women but never mentioned their ceremonial position. However, although she worked in the same area as Eyre, she was there at a later date when enormous changes had already taken place, and she clearly saw her duty as a missionary, not as an ethnographer.

There was less blindness on the part of these early recorders in considering the material culture and the position of women in economic affairs. It is thus possible to say that although the role of women in the ceremonial life was largely ignored and is therefore difficult to reconstruct, their positions in the economic spheres are somewhat easier to define. Although a considerable amount of extrapolation and interpretation is necessary, it is possible to make some assessment of the very substantial role women played in acquiring and preparing food and household utensils.

The important position of women as the economic providers or breadwinners for their husbands and families obviously attracted, indeed concerned English observers who assumed such roles to be the responsibility of men. They considered the importance of women in the economic sphere due not to their skill or independence but to the cruel and savage nature of their husbands. Eyre, although more observant than most, was no exception in his condemnation of the males for allowing their wives to work so hard (Eyre, 1845: 208):

> Like most other savages the Australian looks upon his wife
> as a slave. To her belongs the duty of collecting and preparing
> the daily food, of making the camp or hut for the night, of
> gathering and bringing in firewood, and of procuring water.
> She must also attend to the children, and in travelling carry
> all the moveable property and frequently the weapons for her
> husband. In wet weather she attends to all the outside work,
> whilst her lord and master is snugly seated at the fire.

We might readily ask why Eyre and others saw the position of women as so much inferior to that of white women in their own society. The Aboriginal women, being the major food providers, could be quite independent of their men. Thus when the men went on trading or other expeditions and, later, when they left to work on European farms, the women were quite able to fend for themselves and their children, a situation which would have been envied by many contemporary English women had they understood the reality.

It is evident that Aboriginal women in the south were skilled and experienced food providers. They gathered a variety of foods in a relatively short space of time. The popular view that Aborigines spent all their time in the arduous quest for food is simply not borne out in any of the contemporary records of southern South Australia. Women could obtain all of the necessary food quickly and efficiently. They apparently enjoyed doing so. They worked in groups and evidently had a large amount of fun and comradeship in the process.

In fact, both men and women appeared to enjoy both better food and more leisure time than their contemporaries from Britain who looked down on their lifestyle with such disdain (Eyre, 1845: 253):

> In two or three hours a woman will procure as many fish as
> will last her family for a day. The men are too lazy to do
> anything when food is so abundant, and lie basking under
> the trees in luxurious indolence

Does one detect a slight note of envy in this English gentleman for the 'savages' he has come to protect and civilise?

Women were extremely skilled in the business of earning the daily living. Although early recorders were critical of the high profile women took in such activities and clearly thought men should 'support' their wives in the British tradition, nevertheless such observers could not help but admire the skill, dexterity, speed and obvious enthusiasm women had for their tasks: (Eyre,1845: 267):

> Muscles (sic.) of a very large kind are also got by diving.
> The women whose duty it is to collect these, go into the water
> with small nets (len-ko) hung around their necks, and diving
> to the bottom pick up as many as they can, put them into their
> bags, and rise to the surface for fresh air, repeating the
> operation until their bags have been filled. They have the
> power of remaining for a long time under the water, and
> when they rise to the surface for air, the head and sometimes
> the mouth only is exposed'. . . .

Eyre describes how women caught delicacies like freshwater crayfish (Eyre, 1845: 252) and lobsters (Eyre, 1845: 267). These were group activities for women only.

There are numerous descriptions of fishing of all kinds and of gathering vegetable foods. The women appear to take the major or sole part in such activities. The staple foods are the prerogative of women who are clearly the 'breadwinners' for their families. Although men are not entirely indolent and in fact engage in quite major hunting expeditions for wallabies, kangaroos and birds, these activities provide additional rather than basic foods. As Eyre shows (1845: 283, 287), the women also play a considerable role even in these hunting expeditions, which popular opinion has always assumed to be the sole right of men.

It is difficult to explain the roots of our misconceptions about Aboriginal women. The available evidence all seems to contradict the popular opinions, even to the assumed division between hunting and gathering. Women certainly were the main gatherers, but this does not mean that they were not also engaged in hunting for the larger game.

It is evident that women in southern South Australia played a dominant role in the acquisition of daily food. It is also evident that this was not at the expense of involvement in ceremonial life, either in joint rituals with men, or in distinctly separate 'women's business'. An even cursory glance at the 19th century records questions virtually all of our 20th century assumptions about the role of women in traditional Aboriginal society.

Why, if some women were considered to occupy an insignificant role in society, did they loom so large as such important mythical beings in much of the Dreamtime? Why, if their status was so lowly, did they become so strong and so much in control of their own lives, and those of young people around them, when Europeans arrived? The early historic descriptions of powerful women commanding respect and obedience from men, as well as children, lead us to doubt the accuracy of any view that does not allow such authority in pre-contact times. The old lady at Murray Bridge, for example, known as Queen Monarto, was well respected by all who came into contact with her.

In 1877 an Englishman by the name of Young wrote to the protector of Aborigines requesting a boat for Queen Monarto, apparently on her direction. He wrote: 'I know Her Majesty to be a respectable person and is, I believe, helping to maintain one or two other persons besides herself by fishing' (Government Record Group 52/1/1877/98 Public Record Office, Adelaide). Monarto died in 1890 at a considerable age, having gained considerable authority amongst British as well as Aboriginal residents of the lower Murray. Taplin describes a woman in his diary as 'the most intelligent Aboriginal I ever saw' (25 June, 1859: 13). It is stretching the imagination too much to assume that such women gained stature only after the arrival of European settlers.

The historic records show increasing recognition of women in the post-contact period. Could their rising status really have been due to the 'civilising' effects of the British missionaries and protectors, freeing them from their assumed 'slavery' to their men? It is obviously impossible to determine to what extent the seemingly greater recognition and social power following European settlement was a result of changing circumstances, and to what extent it was largely a continuation of the status of traditional women. It is likely that both factors played a part.

More recent studies from all over Australia (eg. Gale, 1970, 1983) show Aboriginal women in various situations of social and economic power. Cultural continuity is obviously easier to study in central and northern Australia, where change has been more recent and less rapid. Nevertheless, even in southern South Australia there is contemporary evidence of women's significant social position and economic contribution.

I first visited Point McLeay, not as a student of Aboriginal affairs, but as a 15 year-old schoolgirl spending the holidays with my aunt on a nearby property. My aunt played the organ at the church and my uncle went there to hire seasonal labour. At the time I was struck by several of the women with whom my aunt talked. They seemed so outgoing, so much in command, so intelligent and so thirsty for knowledge of the outside world and of the city in particular. At the time, exemption laws were in force and they could not leave the mission without permits. I found their conversation more stimulating than that of most white women. The Aboriginal women at Point McLeay seemed concerned with broader issues of freedom, equality, the validity of Christianity for their situation, the right to employment or social benefits. Admittedly these were not usually expressed in philosophical or political terms but the meaning was clear. Why are we here in this place and what do we do to either improve it or get out of it?

I gathered from my uncle that these issues seemed less important to the men. But the Aboriginal men already had greater freedom. Almost from the beginning of the policy of segregating Aboriginal people on to missions and reserves it was primarily the women who were imprisoned. The men very early were encouraged, indeed usually forced to leave the reserves and their wives and children and go out to work on farms. Here they spent long periods as labourers clearing the land. Point McLeay men also formed shearing teams and moved about the country from one shed to another, often necessitating prolonged absences from their families. When the war came several enlisted and went overseas. Aboriginal men, although often living in harsh conditions, experienced a degree of equality, economic independence and freedom of movement denied to the women.

The women, forced to remain on Point McLeay, were encouraged to find other forms of income. One such industry was basket making. Women had traditionally made baskets of all kinds and there are many records, descriptions and drawings of these baskets in southern South Australia (Eyre, 1845; Angas, 1846). This traditional industry was continued and encouraged by the missionaries to gain much needed money for the missions. Baskets and mats were woven from reeds and rushes by the women and sent to Adelaide for sale (Taplin Diaries, 22 August 1871: 400). Matthews, writing from Manunka mission on 18 April 1902 said: 'Basket and mat making is an industry we encourage here and is even now bringing some income through our dealing with Adelaide and so the natives need not travel to sell them'.

Some years ago I listened to older women, who grew up on Point McLeay, describe the making of baskets and their sale. They recalled memories of the period 1900–1910 when the mission was still in church control. Visitors were encouraged to come and buy baskets, mats and feather dusters and ornaments, as well as to give donations. I was told of the great preparation for these visits, they were after all the only contact most women and children had with the outside world. Children especially were scrubbed up and dressed in their best clothes. As soon as news came that a boat was in sight on the lake children were sent to the wharf to welcome the visitors. These are remembered largely as beautiful ladies in long white dresses who kissed and patted them and usually gave them a penny or two. The handiwork prepared in the days before was also out on display for sale. As one woman recalled: 'Us kids really looked forward to those visits but looking back on it I guess it was really like being in a zoo with people staring at you and talking about what you looked like as if you couldn't hear what they were saying'.

Some women did escape the confines of the mission. They were sent out to work as domestic servants on the surrounding farms and some were even sent to Adelaide. Their stories do not make pretty telling. Whilst some were well treated and given the status of English servants in earlier days, many became little more than slaves, dismissed back to the mission or onto the streets when they became pregnant. Older women have recalled with great emotion, 30 to 40 years after the event, being sent away as young teenagers, expected to work hard and long hours, often at tasks for which they had little training, and not infrequently to be raped by their white bosses. One who at 15 was employed as a cook told me how she had boiling stew poured over her because she had burnt it. Another described the trauma of giving birth to the station owner's child which was taken away immediately so that she could continue her work. As with many such women, she never saw that child again and mourned its loss for many years.

These women were in demand, not only for their sexuality, but also because they brought to difficult and isolated farm kitchens a source of traditional skills. When food was scarce or the flour too full of weevils to make bread they could improvise with some forms of bush tucker and they could make good damper from indigenous plants. Their skills as midwives were also respected. 'On emergencies, native women have sometimes been called in to act as midwives to the wives of white men living in the bush, and have succeeded very well' (Taplin, 1879: 49).

When I returned to Point McLeay in conjunction with field work for my thesis in the 1950s I was able to talk to the older women on a more equal basis. Their main questions to me were about life on 'the outside', especially in the city. Point McLeay had clearly become a prison to many. They felt the urgent need to move away for the sake of their children and grandchildren. They were worried about the low level of education available to them and the lack of employment. Their farm labour was no longer required, as it had been in earlier times, and the market for their craftwork had collapsed. The women were also worried about marriage partners for their children. They had grown up with a deep reverence for the strict marriage rules of their forebears and were very concerned that if they could not leave the mission their children would marry 'too close' or the 'wrong way'.

These discussions and the degree of urgency that accompanied them made me aware of the role of women in organising suitable marriages and maintaining traditional or near traditional marriage rules. They discussed how this marriage was right and that one was wrong.

I do not know what the men talked about when they were alone but all I could gather from white men who worked with them or employed them was a concentration on getting work and money to buy cigarettes and alcohol which was prohibited at the time. The women did talk about the problems of the men drinking and about the white men who smuggled in illicit alcohol. The women felt that the responsibility to maintain 'proper marriage' fell entirely on their shoulders especially since men had become, in their eyes, increasingly irresponsible.

The women also talked about certain myths and it was obvious that even 100 years after the settlement of the mission the women had still been able to pass down at least a few remnants of earlier beliefs and practices. Several of these stories related to death and the part women played both in knowing when a death was imminent and in the site cleansing and mourning ceremonies which followed.

Some families were able to maintain an independent life away from the missions. There were a few areas in the south where this was possible in spite of official attempts to segregate all Aborigines onto missions. A government report of 1899 comments on the removal of several Aborigines from Adelaide and Point McLeay (Government Record Group 52/1/1899/308 Public Record Office). However, at a few points along the Coorong and the lakes, some Aboriginal families obtained land declared as Aboriginal reserve land or inherited it because their white father had been granted the land under a settlement policy entitling white men who married Aboriginal women to certain sections of land. Doreen Kartinyeri recalled several families who 'lived off the land' (Kartinyeri, 1983: 138) to a large degree along the Coorong. When I visited people at such camps in the 1950s there was certainly considerable activity and an atmosphere quite different from the mission. For one thing, the men were present and the families seemed less disrupted than those on the mission. There was work on nearby properties and along the Murray and at the lakes water rats and rabbits were trapped and their skins sold.

I well remember an elderly white haired lady at one of these camps and there was little doubt in my mind that she largely determined the actions and goings and comings of her group and its visitors. It was strong minded women like her who first made me question the subordinate status accredited to Aboriginal women by popular opinion of the time. This question became more focussed as I visited older women in Adelaide, women who had left the mission in the 1950s and set up house in the city. Usually they were without partners of their own age but often ruled a relatively large household, not necessarily all under the one roof. One thing that impressed me immensely was their control over all of the money that came into the household. As a young white woman conscious of my own secondary place in society, I remember being absolutely flabbergasted by the control of such women over their household income and expenditure. Two examples will suffice.

On one occasion I was in the lounge of one house talking to the mother, an Aboriginal woman in her late 50s, when her husband came in and asked her for some money to go and buy cigarettes.

She went out of the room to get the money and gave it to him. As soon as he returned to the house she called out to him to come into the lounge. She interrupted our conversation to ask him to show her the brand of cigarettes and then demanded the change, a few pence, she said would be left on that brand.

On another occasion I was driving an older woman home when she saw her son-in-law and she asked me to turn around to follow him. We drew up alongside of him and she got out and demanded money. He obediently gave her several notes. Later in the car she said it was his pay day and if she did not get the money he would waste it. And he did not even live in the same house as she did. With a certain temerity I asked how and why she had achieved this with such acquiescence on his part, especially as he was employed in the city and living to all outward signs a completely 'assimilated' life. Her power lay apparently not only in her age but also in the large size of her family, its various kin connections and also in the particular relationship he had to her family. I did not understand it but the result was clear. It was also evident to me that even for totally urbanised families, older women had maintained much of their social and economic control of former days, indeed possibly had even enhanced it.

The more I came to know such powerful, active and intelligent Aboriginal women the more I questioned why the government, in all of its emerging training and development schemes for Aborigines, selected men. The white decision-makers, males themselves, were convinced by their belief in their own social 'superiority and absolutely persuaded that in Aboriginal society men are the 'tribal elders', the owners of status and knowledge. So much so that the white administrators sought out Aboriginal men, often with great difficulty, while capable Aboriginal women were passed over.

Aboriginal women, frustrated by the selective grooming of their men, eventually took steps to organise themselves. In Adelaide it was a group of Aboriginal women who set up the first community centre. They acquired a building, raised grants and appointed the first social worker to a solely Aboriginal organisation. From this beginning, they established what was to become the Legal Rights movement in South Australia. It was a women's group in Adelaide that led to the first successful land rights movement in Australia with the passing of the establishment of the Aboriginal Lands Trust in 1966. It was a city-based women's group that established the land rights support meetings to assist in the traditional land claims of the Pitjantjatjara people in South Australia. Not surprisingly, it was a woman from the south of the State who became the first qualified Aboriginal lawyer in South Australia.

The paradox is still with us today.

## Acknowledgements

I am especially grateful to Caroline Laurence, who undertook the archival research necessary for this paper.

## References

Angas, G.F. (1846) *South Australia Illustrated* London: Thomas McLean

Bell, D. (1983) 'Consulting with women' in F. Gale ed. *We are Bosses Ourselves: The Role and Status of Aboriginal Women Today* Canberra: Australian Institute of Aboriginal Studies

Campbell, T.D. (1934) Notes on the Aborigines of the South-East of South Australia, Part 1, *Transactions of the Royal Society of SA* 58, pp. 22–32

Cawthorne, W.A (1844) Rough Notes on the Manners and Customs of the Natives, reprinted in *Proceedings of the Royal Geographic Society of S.A* 1926, 26, pp. 47–77

Eyre, E.J. (1845) *Journals of Expeditions of Discovery into Central Australia and Overland* Vol. 2, London: T. and W. Boone

Gale, F. ed. (1970) *Women's Role in Aboriginal Society* Canberra: Australian Institute of Aboriginal Studies

Gale, F. ed. (1983) *We are Bosses Ourselves: The Role and Status of Aboriginal Women Today* Canberra: Australian Institute of Aboriginal Studies

Kartinyeri, D. (1983) 'Recording our History' in F. Gale (ed.) *We are Bosses Ourselves: The Role and Status of Aboriginal Women Today* Canberra: Australian Institute of Aboriginal Studies

Matthews, J (1902) Letter from Manunka Mission to the Minister of Education, Public Record Office, Adelaide, G.R.G. 52/1/1902/132

Smith, Mrs. J. (1880) *The Booandik Tribe of South Australian Aborigines: A Sketch of Their Habits, Customs, Legends and Language* Adelaide: E. Spiller, Government Printer

Stephens, J. (1839) 'Adelaide and Encounter Bay Tribes' reprinted in J.A. Parkhouse (1923) *Reprints and Papers Relating to the Autochthones of Australia* Vol. 1 Parkhouse and Woodville, South Australia

Taplin, G. Diaries, 4th April 1859—19th June 1879, 3 Volumes. Mortlock Library of South Australiana. Typescript P.R.G. 186/1/3

—— (1879) ed. *The Folklore, Manners, Customs and Language of the South Australian Aborigines* Adelaide: Government Printer

# Index